Craft
BEER
London

D1142655

Written & Compiled by
WILL HAWKES

Photography by
LUCA SAGE & JAMES LAMBIE

First published in the UK by Vespertine Press 2012

Copyright Vespertine Press 2012
Text copyright Will Hawkes

Photography copyright Luca Sage & James Lambie
Additional images courtesy of Fuller, Smith and Turner PLC (Chiswick) ©
and Truman's (Black Eagle Brewery Ltd.) ©

A catalogue of this book is available from the British Library

ISBN 978-0-9566582-3-4

Design & cover by Matt Barker at Artwerk.co.uk
Icon design by Gavin Lucas
Digital mapping by Encompass Graphics Ltd, Hove, UK
www.encompass-graphics.co.uk

Printed and bound in the UK by Four Corners Print
This book has been printed on paper produced by sustainably managed forests.

All rights reserved, which includes the right to reproduce this book or portions
thereof in any form whatsoever without the prior written permission of the publishers.

Set in TR Avalon, **U.S. 101** & *English*

Also available from Vespertine Press -
The Independent Coffee Book London
& *The Wellbeing Guide to London*

www.vespertinepress.co.uk

CONTENTS

Central

North

East

South / South East

West / South West

Craft Beer Companion

USING THIS GUIDE

The first part of this book serves as a guide to the foremost craft beer pubs, bars and breweries in London. They are divided into five key areas comprising Central, North, East, South / South East and West / South West, allowing you to easily find these places depending on your location. At the end of each area section there are listings of other great craft beer locations that we also recommend you visit.

There are two page styles distinguishing pubs and breweries, each containing key information such as train and bus routes, opening hours and contact details. (Please note: whilst we have done our very best to keep all of this information current, there may be unforeseeable changes made to these details during the lifespan of this book. The bus and train routes listed are suggestions only and other lines or routes may serve your journey more effectively. If in doubt, contact the pub or brewery directly and refer to the TFL website for changes to scheduled transport.)

The second part of this book is a Craft Beer Companion, comprising information about craft beer, its history and its place in London today. Finally, at the back of the book you will find a fold-out map of London, detailing the areas both North and South of the River Thames.

The following logos appear within the guide. They denote:

 Craft Beer Brewery

 Craft Beer Shop

FOREWORD

by
Evin O'Riordain
THE KERNEL

It is the only story – the story of birth, then loss and then rediscovery. Our concern here is that story of beer in London; of the brewing and the drinking of beer. Here once, and for a long period of time, was the brewing centre of the world, the birthplace of now worldly beer styles, a template for the processes of industrialisation. Beer on a grand scale. Here faded, over a long period of time, the consideration of beer as in any way essential to the existence of the city. We had become, three years ago, a city with nine breweries. Nor was this a place noted for drinking good beer. These lengths of time are periods we cannot comprehend, and the forces that motivated these changes have become obscured.

And then change again. A recent resurgence in brewing here. Smaller, now, with a change in emphasis on what it means to brew. A boom in the availability of good beer. A shift in perspective on the part of those that drink – considerations of quality become paramount. Care is being taken. Focus has sharpened. Something is happening on the ground. The timescale is a scant three years. The beginnings of a revitalisation. Is it one tied to a rebirth of London's traditions? Or an influx of new ideas, inspirations and attitudes from elsewhere? What place does beer hold here and now?

As of yet we do not know. But we have it in our hands to make something of it. We are in the midst of a struggle, the struggle over the meaning of what we see, the question of what beer means in London. There is still only a tiny amount of good beer being sold and drunk here. We see here in this book a mapping of the present outposts of this wave of good beer.

The signs of changes of attitude toward the beer, towards its brewing, and its drinking. People are taking care over what they drink. As with what they eat. But we must still wage war against the massive amounts of bad beer being drunk. And bad places to drink it in, places hostile to all that makes beer alive. We do this by championing the cause of quality. By drinking good beer.

We exist in a present which has yet to be determined. We are the ones with the ability to make something happen, to define how fundamental this shift is. This book is an image, a cross section, of something growing in London. We cannot yet define what. But take this as a point of departure, and use it to explore the question. Let your actions help those in the future define what beer means in London in 2012.

WHAT IS CRAFT BEER?

by
Will Hawkes

What is craft beer? It depends who you ask. For some drinkers, it's a movement that has revolutionised the brewing world with its insistence that beer must be, above all else, full-flavoured and interesting. For others, it's a rather ambiguous term which merely serves to obscure what really matters about a beer – whether it tastes good or bad. It is probably worth pointing out that those who take the second view tend to be rather longer in the tooth than craft beer's proponents.

For all their drinking experience, though, these craft deniers often miss the point. Something has happened to beer over the past few years, something that has changed the way we see this most democratic of alcoholic drinks: beer lovers have been enfranchised. It is now possible to get good beer in parts of the world where, just ten years ago, industrially-produced lager would have been your only option. The craft-brewing movement has torn down barriers, bringing brewers closer to drinkers and ensuring that nothing is verboten. Why shouldn't a brewery in Windsor produce a Pilsner every bit as good as one made in Pilsen, for example?

It is perhaps this challenge to the old order that most offends those who rail against the term 'craft' but they have nothing to worry about. The new school of brewers have huge respect for tradition. Anyone who has heard Meantime founder and head brewer Alastair Hook talk about Bavaria knows that this is a man who, for all of his desire to change Britain's drinking culture, loves tradition.

Craft beer (or, perhaps more accurately, craft brewing) is a state of mind rather than something that can be exactly defined. Like jazz, perhaps (and like the word jazz, it's hard to know who coined the term 'craft beer', although it may have been legendary beer writer and Yorkshireman Michael Jackson). Bob Pease, Chief Operating Officer at the American Brewers' Association (whose website carries a definition which requires the brewery to be small, independent and traditional; 'small' and 'traditional', of course, mean something different in the US), believes it is about a certain approach.

"Authenticity is the key to our movement's success," he says. "Consumers want a product that they can feel good about purchasing. The people that are behind craft brewing in the US are as authentic, as real and as passionate as you get. And that really comes across."

Of course, there is more to craft beer than a row about semantics. Craft beer has a fascinating history of its own, which began in the mid-1970s in California. Sick of the insipid industrial brews that dominated the American market at the time, a group of renegades (think the A Team, but with hops) decided to do something about it. Doug Odell, who went on to found the hugely respected Colorado brewery Odell, was one of them.

"We lived in this huge city (Los Angeles) but I had to drive thirty miles to get to the nearest shop where I could buy homebrewing equipment," he once told me. "The ingredients were really basic – you'd buy a bag of hops but it wouldn't tell you what they were, how strong they were. The beers were pretty bad but I stuck with it.

"What really opened it up for us was that the US brewing business was in rapid consolidation, starting from the end of the 60s. They all made the same kind of beer – that American lager. There was an opening. It started with entrepreneurs, home brewers whose friends told them they were making pretty good beer so they decided to go commercial. I was one of those."

Ken Grossman, perhaps the most important figure in the short history of craft beer, had a similar experience. He founded Sierra Nevada in 1979; just over thirty years later, its most famous product (Sierra Nevada Pale Ale) can be sampled all over the world, including London. Sierra Nevada was one of three hugely influential Northern Californian breweries: the others were Anchor in San Francisco (which inspired Sierra Nevada and many others, having been taken over by Fritz Maytag in 1965) and New Albion which, sadly, lasted just six years but played a key role in starting the process of changing how Americans viewed beer. They were inspired by the traditional beers of England such as pale ale and porter.

Interestingly, a group of righteous malcontents had experienced a similar sensation in the UK a few years earlier, but their response was different: they founded the Campaign for Real Ale. The desire of the big brewers to cut costs had led to the rise of insipid keg beer – which was nothing like the full-flavoured stuff you can buy today from the likes of Camden Town and The Kernel. In response, CAMRA was formed and, slowly but surely, an effective fightback (a counter-revolution, if you like) began.

This was a (hugely successful) campaign to protect traditional British ale. Craft beer, as we have already seen, is less respectful of national boundaries; it landed in the UK in the 1990s but it was not until Meantime

(founded in 2000) that there was a brewery who seemed committed to breaking the "cask ale = all good beer" equation that dominated British drinking. For a long time, they ploughed a lone furrow, but the penny has finally dropped. Breweries are opening across the UK that hew closely to the craft beer ethos. In the 1980s, new British microbreweries would make British beer, largely bitter ale: now they take on all manner of styles.

We can expect that process to continue. London has finally woken up to the craft beer revolution: like a particularly malignant rash (but with more pleasing consequences), craft beer pubs are spreading across London, starting in the East. As we have seen, breweries are also popping up all over – including in the West of the city, which has yet to fully embrace craft beer. That will come, particularly as Fuller's, that titan of West London ale, have shown their open-mindedness with the creation of the Union Tavern, which showcases the best London beer. Craft beer has taken a long time to take hold in the capital but the events of the past two years suggest that there is no looking back.

Central

EUSTON TAP

190 Euston Road NW1 2EF
Tel: 020 3137 8837

Central

Hours	Mon-Sat: 12-11.30 Sun: 12-10.30	Trains	Euston Tube & Rail
Online	@eustontap eustontap.com	Buses	Routes 10, 18, 30, 59, 68, 73 - Euston Station

What to Drink	Food
Thornbridge & Magic Rock	Pizza

The Euston Arch was torn down in 1961. Despite a campaign led by Sir John Betjeman and Nikolaus Pevsner, the Conservative government of the time decided that a structure which had gazed over this corner of central London for more than one hundred and twenty years had no further use. Nothing was left of the Arch (many of the stones that made up the Arch were later discovered at the bottom of a canal in East London) except two lodges that had stood either side.

There is a happy ending to this story, however. Longstanding plans to have the Arch rebuilt are still floating around and one of those lodges that escaped demolition now houses the Euston Tap. Like the station itself, the Tap is a portal for Northern ideas in the capital; it is the younger sibling of the Sheffield Tap, a pub at the railway station in that Yorkshire city. And like the Sheffield Tap, it is a place where you can expect to find superb beer, even if it lacks the easy conviviality of its Northern counterpart.

Perhaps being housed in a lodge designed for an entirely different purpose best explains this. Downstairs you'll find a bar and upstairs you'll find the seating, which is a slightly unsatisfactory arrangement, but needs must. Besides, the long bar downstairs is well worth propping up as you inspect the magnificent array of beer taps arranged on the back wall, or the vast selection of bottles in the Tap's two sizeable fridges.

And if you want more than that – who are you, Oliver Twist? – then a quick stroll across to the other gatehouse is in order. There you'll find the Cider Tap, probably London's premier cider drinking spot. Great beer, great cider: if only Betjeman had use of a time machine, he might not have groused so much about the end of the Arch. At the very least, he could have drowned his sorrows in majestic style.

THE QUEEN'S HEAD

66 Acton Street WC1X 9NB
Tel: 020 7713 5772

Hours	Tues-Sat: 12-12	Trains	King's Cross Tube & Rail
Online	@thequeens_head queensheadlondon.com	Buses	Routes 17, 45, 46 Acton Street

Central

What to Drink
Saison Dupont

Food
Bar food - pork pies and good British cheese

It's impossible to walk into The Queen's Head and not wish this was your local. Sure, it hasn't got the widest selection of beers in the capital but everything on offer seems so well chosen. The handpumps might include Kentish icons Gadd's, Bristol Beer Factory or Dark Star, while those with more continental tastes can choose between a bottle of the magnificent Saison Dupont or Kriek Boon on tap.

Beer, of course, is not everything: atmosphere matters, too. On a rain-lashed evening a few months back, the place was alive with young and not-so-young drinkers chatting happily. There was the sort of buzz that pubs only get when people are genuinely happy to be there. And it's easy to be happy at the Queen's Head.

Everything here is near pitch-perfect, like the beer-friendly food (pork pies, meat platters and cheese boards) or the beautifully engraved front window. The bar staff are welcoming and the other alcohol-based offerings - wine, whisky, et al - look pretty damn good, too. On top of all that there is regular music, although it should be noted that sometimes that music is jazz. Well, nowhere is perfect.

HOLBORN WHIPPET

25-29 Sicilian Avenue, Holborn WC1A 2QH
Tel: 020 3137 9937

Hours	Mon-Sun: 11-1	Trains	Holborn Tube
Online	@holbornwhippet holbornwhippet.com	Buses	Routes 8, 25, 242, 521, N8 – Holborn Station

What to Drink	Food
Something sparkled	Charcoal-grilled meats

Life can be tough in the big city for homesick Northerners. No one wants to chat on the bus, the fish and chips are rubbish and everyone thinks you wear clogs at home. Thank God, then, for this refuge (of sorts), which has just opened up in Holborn. It's even named after the official animal of the North - the whippet. What's more, the beer is often served the 'proper' way, through a sparkler, so the head is good and creamy. And Southerners who complain about it can go and cry into their naturally-conditioned booze.

Of course, there are some legitimate concerns about sparkling but this is not the place to air them. What's important is that the Holborn Whippet is bringing a little variety to the London beer market and variety, I think we all agree, is good.

This variety extends to the other beers on offer, such as hoppy keg offerings and high-quality continental lagers (even if the lack of bottled beers is a bit of a drawback). What's more, Holborn Whippet is one of very few craft beer spots in the centre of town, which is dominated by tourist-friendly venues serving the same bland beers. Even sparkler-phobic Southerners, then, should raise a glass to the Whippet.

EXMOUTH ARMS

23 Exmouth Market EC1R 4QL
Tel: 020 3551 4772

Hours	Mon-Thurs: 11-12	**Trains**	Farringdon Rail
	Fri & Sat: 11-1.30		
	Sun: 11-10.30	**Buses**	19, 38, 341, N19, N38,
			N41 – Tysoe Street
Online	@exmoutharms		
	exmoutharms.com		

What to Drink
Camden Town, Oakham, Brooklyn

Food
Sliders – or mini-Hamburgers, as your Nan would have known them

This has always been a beautiful pub on the outside (check out that green Courage tiling), but it now looks good on the inside too. The Exmouth Arms is another of 2012's remarkable crop of new craft beer pubs and its emergence makes this corner of Central / East London perhaps the best place for a pub crawl in the city. A short tour around these ends will take in the Exmouth, Craft Beer Co., The Old Red Cow and plenty of other good boozers besides.

But you might just decide to sample The Exmouth Arms, and that would be a perfectly good plan. The pub is placed on Exmouth Market, where a food market operates every Friday and Saturday, making this quite the spot for a pub that takes beer seriously. Indeed, it's hard to think of anywhere more suitable for a craft beer makeover. Exmouth Market already boasted the likes of Spanish restaurant Moro and table football shrine Cafe Kick; now it's got the sort of beer venue it was crying out for. A beautiful pub on a beautiful street selling lots of beautiful beer: well, what are you waiting for?

CRAFT BEER CO.

82 Leather Lane, Clerkenwell EC1N 7TR

Hours	Mon-Sat: 12-11 Sun: 12-10.30	Trains	Farringdon Rail
Online	@thecraftbeerco thecraftbeerco.com	Buses	Routes 55, 243, N35, N55 - Hatton Garden

What to Drink
Try the house lager from Mikkeller or the ale from Kent Brewery

Food
Excellent pork pies and Scotch eggs

This is where London's beer tribes meet. Sidle up to the bar and you might find yourself wedged in between a densely-bearded man of a certain age and a hip young gun-slinger: such is the inclusivity of a place that may be expensive but, when it comes to beer, has something for everyone.

The house offerings, for example, couldn't be more varied. Clerkenwell Pale Ale, which is brewed down in the heart of England's hop county by the Kent Brewery, is supremely drinkable stuff that is packed with restrained citrus bitterness. It's the sort of beer that would please anyone, which perhaps can't be said of the house lager. That particular beast comes courtesy of Danish gypsy brewers Mikkeller, by most measures the leading light in Europe's craft beer movement. Forget all you know about lager: this is bracingly bitter and strong with the sort of citrus bite you'd normally associate with a West Coast IPA.

There's plenty more variety to choose from at the bar too, catering for those who like it sour - spontaneous fermentation is the only type of fermentation for London's more discerning drinkers - to those whose idea of heaven is a gentle, elegantly balanced mild. There are sixteen hand pumps in all, plenty more keg beer and over four hundred bottles to choose from. Craft Beer Co. also regularly features the likes of Thornbridge and Dark Star, often regarded as the Northern and Southern contenders for Britain's craft beer heavyweight title.

What is perhaps most impressive about Craft Beer Co. isn't just the choice on offer, it's also the outstanding quality that's on show too. Their attention to sourcing and collaboration with some of the world's finest micro-breweries have won Craft Beer Co. notable acclaim in the mainstream press and even the sensational (if not slightly dubious) award of 4th Best Bar in the World on RateBeer.com.

All this hype and a list of choices that puts most other pubs to shame can be rather overwhelming, of course. You may need something to cling to as you survey a beer selection that could intimidate the most self-assured of beer drinkers. But fear not: Look to the far end of the bar where a glass dome houses some of the best pork pies and Scotch eggs in town. There's your ballast. Now all you need to do is pick a beer.

THE OLD RED COW

71-72 Long Lane, Smithfield EC1A 9EJ
Tel: 020 7726 2595

Central

Hours	Mon-Thurs: 12-11	Trains	Barbican Tube /
	Fri & Sat: 12-12		Farringdon
	Sun: 12-10.30		
		Buses	Routes 55, 63, 153
Online	@oldredcow		Barbican Station
	theoldredcow.com		

| What to Drink | The Kernel, | Food | High-quality pub grub |
| Redemption, Camden Town | | | e.g. top-notch Scotch eggs |

There aren't that many neighbourhoods where you can still get a flavour of the old London. Many of the great market places, like Covent Garden - now a glorified shopping centre - or Spitalfields, have been neutered by the unwelcome attention of modernity. Be thankful, then, for Smithfield, which still resists the march of time. This is where meat has been bought and sold for over eight hundred years. It's a unique spot now, and all the more precious for it.

Being a market, it is surrounded by good places for a beer but the Old Red Cow is probably the best if you're looking for variety, guaranteed quality and a soupçon of modernity. This is an up-to-date-looking place, but given the commitment to quality beer and food, that shouldn't be a problem for anyone. This interest in beer and food carries over into the dinners hosted by The Old Red Cow on an occasional basis. For example, in April 2012 the beer of Tottenham's Redemption was matched with all manner of delicious grub. How does duck with spiced honey & figs served with a glass of Redemption's complex, spicy Urban Dusk sound? Good? Then the Old Red Cow is the place for you.

THE OLD FOUNTAIN

3 Baldwin Street EC1V 9NU
Tel: 020 7253 2970

Central

Hours	Mon-Fri: 11-11	Trains	Old Street Tube
	Sat: 12-11		
	Sun: 12-10	Buses	Routes 43, 205, 214
			Old Street Station
Online	@OldFountainAles		
	oldfountain.co.uk		

What to Drink
Dark Star

Food
Simple pub grub like cheese
and salt beef sandwiches

As a refuge from the end-of-days hell scene that is Old Street Tube, The Old Fountain can't be bettered. This welcoming pub has been cheering up harassed drinkers for generations but, in terms of beer, they've never had it so good as they do now. You can expect to find The Kernel, Dark Star and Brodie's here on a regular basis. Even if there was no other beer, this would be a place worth going out of your way to visit.

Of course, there is other beer, but there's something else that sets this place apart. This is a family-run pub and has been for almost fifty years. Just think of the changes that have overtaken London and its pubs since 1964, the year that the Durrant family took charge of The Old Fountain. Those were the days before the Campaign for Real Ale existed, let alone craft beer; an era when virtually all beer in the US had about as much character as a can of fizzy pop. So don't come here for a fancy interior or a beer cocktail. Do, however, visit The Old Fountain for great ales and a taste of London's pub history.

LISTINGS
OTHER CENTRAL CRAFT BEER DESTINATIONS

THE ALBANY
240 Great Portland Street W1W 5QU
Tel: 020 7387 0221
Online: thealbanyw1w.co.uk
@thealbany
Mon–Sat: 12pm - 12am
Sun: 12pm - 10.30pm

THE CROWN & TWO CHAIRMEN
32 Dean Street, Soho W1D 3SB
Tel: 020 7437 8192
Online: thecrownandtwochairmenw1.co.uk
Mon-Thurs: 12pm - 11.30pm
Fri & Sat: 12pm - 12am
Sun: 12 - 10.30pm

THE HARP
47 Chandos Place, Covent Garden WC2N 4HS
Tel: 020 7836 0291
Online: harpcoventgarden.com
@harppub
Mon: 10.30am - 11pm
Tue-Sat: 10.30am - 11.30pm
Sun: 12pm - 10.30pm

THE OLD COFFEE HOUSE

49 Beak Street, Soho W1F 9SF
Tel: 020 7437 2197
Mon-Sat: 11am - 11pm
Sun: 12pm - 10.30pm

THE CROSS KEYS

31 Endell Street, Covent Garden WC2H 9BA
Tel: 020 7836 5185
Online: crosskeyscoventgarden.com
Mon-Sat: 11am - 11pm
Sun: 12pm - 10.30pm

THE GUNMAKERS

13 Eyre Street Hill, Clerkenwell EC1R 5ET
Tel: 020 7278 1022
Online: thegunmakers.co.uk
@thegunmakers
Mon-Fri: 12pm - 11pm

JERUSALEM TAVERN

55 Britton Street, Clerkenwell EC1M 5UQ
Tel: 020 7490 4281
Online: stpetersbrewery.co.uk/london
@jerusalemtavern
Mon-Fri: 11am - 11pm

THE FOX AND ANCHOR

115 Charterhouse Street EC1M 6AA
Tel: 020 7250 1300
Online: foxandanchor.com
@foxandanchorpub
Mon-Fri : 7am - 11pm
Sat: 8.30am - 11pm
Sun: 8.30am - 10pm

North

THE HORSESHOE

28 Heath Street, Hampstead NW3 6TE

North

Hours	Mon-Thurs: 10-11 Fri & Sat: 10-12 Sun: 10-10.30	Trains	Hampstead Underground
Online thehorseshoehampstead.com		Buses	Routes 46, 268, N5 Hampstead Station

What to Drink Camden Town	Food Excellent gastro fare

Hampstead feels like another world. Having clambered out of the Tube, you're greeted by somewhere that, in appearance at least, has more in common with Tunbridge Wells than the capital. It's so clean, so well-kempt, so very slightly unnerving. Thank God, then, that Hampstead is also home to The Horseshoe - there can't be many pubs in Tunbridge Wells like this.

For a start, there used to be a brewery downstairs where Jasper Cuppaidge, the man behind the Camden Town brewery, cut his brewing teeth. Camden Town Brewery pays homage to these beginnings by incorporating a horseshoe on its logo, and while there's no beer brewed on site anymore, The Horseshoe is tantamount to being a Camden Town brewery tap as you'll always find four or five of their beers here. The pub also carries excellent beers from slightly further afield meaning that the handpumps might feature Tottenham's Redemption or Windsor and Eton, and keg options often include Sierra Nevada and Little Creatures Pale Ale - the elderflower-scented classic from Cuppaidge's home nation, Australia.

This is a place where beer is afforded the same respect as wine, so there are blackboards behind the bar devoted to each drink. The wine range, needless to say, is excellent although there's plenty of beers to be getting on with before you resort to the grape.

The Horseshoe looks great too. The whitewashed walls and high ceiling give it a real sense of space, which is only right: this is Hampstead, after all, where North London comes to breathe. That Hampstead virtue is reflected in how clean The Horseshoe feels. That's important, because if a pub is grubby you can't help worrying about how well the beer pipes are looked after. You need have no such fears here.

All this, and decent grub too. The Horseshoe's commitment to interesting eating was demonstrated when they took part in the London Brewers' Alliance trip to Kent to pick hop shoots back in April 2012. Hop shoots (the young tip of the hop) are a delicious, somewhat forgotten food in this country, sometimes called poor man's asparagus. The Horseshoe was one of a number of places around London that raced the hop shoots back to town and put them straight on the menu.

And what did The Horsehoe make with their Kentish bounty? Whole plaice with hop shoots, Blythburgh pork chop and hop shoots and a Saturday brunch of Kent hop shoots, poached egg, English muffin and hollandaise sauce. A pint of Camden Pale Ale and a plate of hop shoots - you'd journey to Tunbridge Wells for that.

THE SOUTHAMPTON ARMS

139 Highgate Road NW5 1LE
Tel: 07958 780 073

Hours	Mon-Sun: 12-11 or 12	Trains	Gospel Oak Tube & Overground
Online	@southamptonnw5 thesouthamptonarms.co.uk	Buses	Routes 214, C2 Dartmouth Park Road

What to Drink	Food
Everything is good here so try something new	Pork baps and other pork products

From the self-consciously spit-and-sawdust interior you might imagine that The Southampton Arms has been here since Churchill was in charge and Britannia still just about ruled the waves. You'd be mistaken. This Gospel Oak pub opened in 2009 and, for all its old-school touches, it appears to have captured the zeitgeist: a spate of similar beer-focused boozers have sprung up across London in its wake. When you cross the threshold of this special little pub, you're looking at the future, not the past.

This is down to The Southampton Arms' belief in quality: you'll only find beers and ciders from small, independent British producers here, which means lots of Dark Star, Crouch Vale, Summer Wine and Gadds', to name but four regulars. You're more likely to find a pina colada than a poor-quality pint on the bar. As important as the quality of the beer, though, is the quality of the atmosphere. This is a place where you can really take your time and enjoy an afternoon pint (or three) as the sun streams in through the big window at the front. Perhaps that's because it's such a simple place: good beer, basic fittings, cash only at the bar.

It's a pretty small pub, too, so if you're coming of an evening (and it doesn't have to be Friday or Saturday) make sure you get here early. It can get busy. That's a good thing though, even if you have to stand - better to stand in a tiny, soulful boozer like this than to sit in one of central London's drinking barns. There are plenty of appealing touches to take in here, like the elegant white tiled wall behind the bar, the small open fire or the old piano which competes with a record player in providing the pub's soundtrack.

Then there's the food. If the thought of all that magnificent beer wasn't enough to make you jump up and make for Gospel Oak, then how about The Southampton Arms' array of pies, pork baps and Scotch eggs? Like the beer selection, there's something remarkably refreshing about a pub that refuses to compromise on food. If you like pork, you're in hog heaven. If you don't, there's always the beer.

More than anything, The Southampton Arms is a magnificent riposte to the idea that there's no place for an old-school pub in modern London. Pubs need something more than just beer and bar snacks, we're told, if they're to survive in an age when people have many more leisure options. The Southampton Arms presents a forceful counter-argument. What you really need is great beer and a good atmosphere, and then everyone - from your grandad to your craft-loving 23-year-old cousin – will be happy. Let's hope that is the future.

ALE
CIDER
MEAT

AL ALE

REAL ALE

SOUTHAMPTON ARMS

REAL CIDER

ALE
&
CIDER
HOUSE

Estate Ag

CAMDEN TOWN BREWERY

55-59 Wilkin Street Mews NW5 3NN
www.camdentownbrewery.com

Hours	Look out for
Thurs: 12-10, Fri: 12-11, Sat: 12-10	Camden Ink stout

There's a puritan distaste for marketing among some beer drinkers. Anything that looks sharper than Johnny Vegas in a hessian sack is treated with suspicion; if it's shiny and appealing, it's probably because the beer is rubbish. Now, there's plenty of evidence to suggest they might have a point (check the marketing budgets of the big lager brands) but there's also some compelling counter-arguments. Exhibit one: Camden Town.

Everything about this operation is sharp and modern: the high-tech brewing equipment, the branded hoodies worn by the employees and the new brewery bar which opened in April, for example. But more importantly, the beer is always a pleasure to drink and approachable, too. The Hells is crisp and clean, the Pale Ale has a subtle citrus kick and the wheat beer is satisfyingly full-bodied. Best of all is the coffee-tinged Camden Ink, one of a spate of stouts currently giving Guinness cause for concern around the country.

Camden's stock beers are all modern interpretations of classic styles, as is the beer they dreamt up for this past Olympic summer. Camden 1908, a beer brewed using a recipe from another long-defunct Camden-based brewery, was a delicious response to the problem all brewers faced in 2012: how do we celebrate this momentous year in an interesting, unique way? Very few brewers, if any, managed it with the bravado and panache that Camden displayed.

But whilst Camden Town are clearly proud Londoners, there are also recognisable hallmarks of a strong American influence in everything they do. Camden's Australian founder Jasper Cuppaidge is a self-proclaimed fan of Sierra Nevada, one of the breweries that kick-started the craft beer revolution in Northern California during the early 1980s. Jasper was the boss at Hampstead's Horseshoe pub before Camden Town was born and it was there that he witnessed his customers' passion for Sierra Nevada Pale Ale. It was this interest in a (then) little-known beer from far, far away, that helped convince him the time was right for a craft beer revolution in London.

Sierra Nevada is not the only American brewer that Camden Town is enamoured of, though. In August 2012, Bill Graham from Colorado's Ska Brewing came to London to do some drinking and to introduce the natives to his magnificent wares during a tap takeover at Camden Town. He followed that up by brewing a special beer with the Camden boys that was a blend of Camden Town Hells and Ska's Modus Hoperandi IPA. Definitely one to look out for.

This American approach also manifests itself in how Camden engage with their customers. There's plenty of social media activity and, thanks to the brewery bar and regular tours of the premises, drinkers are kept right up to date with what's going on. In fact, there's only one thing that isn't clear about Camden Town. Why is the brewery in Kentish Town?

THE BLACK HEART

3 Greenland Place, Camden NW1 0AP
Tel: 020 7428 9730

Hours	Mon-Tues: 3-11:30	Trains	Camden Town Tube
	Weds-Thurs: 3-12		
	Friday: 12-2	Buses	Routes 24, 27, 31,
	Sunday: 12-11		168, N5, N28
			Camden Town
Online	@theblack_heart		Station
	ourblackheart.com		

What to Drink	Food
Moor	Pizza

The Black Heart might be a bit of a shock for those who harbour preconceptions about beer and the people who drink it. This place rocks, and not in the sense that the foundations are faulty. No; the jukebox is stacked with great tunes and they put on regular gigs here. And unlike most venues in London, the beer is excellent.

It's not that unlikely a combination, when you think about it, and particularly not in Camden. This is a part of town that likes to think of itself as a little edgier than your average neighbourhood, even if the real action has moved elsewhere since those heady mid-Nineties days when the pop world gathered in The Good Mixer. Some of that spirit remains, though, and it can be found at the Black Heart, as can any number of interesting brews. You might find something from Somerset's Moor Beer among the impressive selection of bottles in the fridge. Moor is run by Justin Hawke, a Californian with a deep love for hops. And right now, what's more rock and roll than hops?

THIS WEEKS SPECIAL BREWS
MOOR BEER COMPANY
NATURAL BEAUTY   £3.90
NOR'HOP   £4.00

BY THE HORNS
STIFF UPPER LIP   £3.90

LONDON FIELDS BREWERY
PALE ALE   £3.90
WILDINE
IMPERIAL BROWN ALE £3.90

BREWDOG

113 Bayham Street, Camden NW1 0AG
Tel: 020 7284 4626

North

Hours	Mon-Thurs: 12-11.30	Trains	Camden Town Tube
	Fri-Sat: 12-12		
	Sun: 12-10.30	Buses	Routes 31, N28, N31
			Bayham Street, or
Online	@BrewDogCamden		alight at Camden
	www.brewdog.com/		Town Tube
	bars/camden		

What to Drink	Food
Brewdog, obviously, or Mikkeller	Pizza and burgers

It's only right that BrewDog's flagship beer is called Punk: not since the days of Johnny Rotten and his sneering, gobbing pals has an upstart newcomer so expertly upset the established order. It was also particularly fitting that BrewDog chose a tank to publicise the opening of this, their first bar in London. That's about as subtle as marketing gets for the Aberdeen outfit, and thousands of drinkers adore them for it.

One of the first things most beer lovers will notice about the bar is the lack of hand pumps. There is no real ale in BrewDog-land, at least not since the end of 2011 when they decided to stop making it. What they may lack in real ale they more than make up for in other ways, however. The bar boasts some of the best craft beer on the planet, not only from BrewDog but from other modern brewing superstars like Mikkeller, Stone and Hitachino Nest. Expect big flavours and fairly big prices. If that doesn't sound like your cup of tea, then think again. BrewDog's bars are a winning combination of über-hip beer choices and friendly, genuinely helpful bar staff.

No one need feel they're not welcome here and any questions will be willingly fielded: BrewDog are recruiting for the craft beer revolution and you don't have to be under thirty to apply. Nonetheless, what with the bar's location and BrewDog's reputation, this place is generally filled with more youthful boozers come Friday and Saturday night.

That's a sign of the incredible progress BrewDog have made since they got going back in 2007. They've upset plenty of people along the way (James Watt, co-founder of BrewDog, surely wouldn't have it any other way) but their passion cannot be doubted. The truth is that they've kicked down the door and plenty of others, including many of London's newer brewers, have followed. Britain's beer landscape is being transformed and few have had more to do with that than BrewDog. You can buy Punk IPA in most supermarkets now - who knows what else you'll be able to get in a couple of years' time?

It's hard to overstate how popular the Scottish scamps are with those who (for whatever reason) can't get on with Britain's traditional real ale scene. And while the loyalty they inspire can be a little over the top at times, you have to admire their courage. Plenty of risks have been taken by BrewDog since their formation and the beneficiary has been British beer.

For all that, there is one criticism you could level at BrewDog's Camden outlet: it's too small. No need to worry, though, as the second BrewDog bar in the capital has just opened in Shoreditch. BrewDog's tank may have rolled into Camden back in 2011 but it's unlikely to stop there.

REDEMPTION BREWERY

Compass West Industrial Estate, West Road, Tottenham N17 0XL
www.redemptionbrewing.co.uk

Hours	By appointment only	What to Drink	Trinity

Tottenham is no longer chiefly famous for an underachieving football team: now it's got an overachieving brewery. Redemption was founded in 2010 by Andy Moffat (described by one in-the-know brewer as 'the nicest man in brewing') and has gone from strength to strength since. Many of the best pubs in London seem to have Redemption's beers on more often than not – a tribute to how well Moffat and his crew have done in marrying Britain's traditional cask beer to craft-beer open-mindedness.

You can see this with one of Redemption's most lauded beers, Trinity, which is in the best of British traditions: low in alcohol (3 per cent) but complex and satisfying nonetheless. It's no exaggeration to say that there aren't many brewers – even those whose products are lauded around the globe – who could match that.

Moffat, then, has good reason to be thankful of his decision to quit The City for a life in brewing. His beers have quickly become an integral part of the London scene: as integral, perhaps, as a late-season slump from Tottenham Hotspur.

THE JOLLY BUTCHERS

204 Stoke Newington High Street N16 7HU
Tel: 020 7249 9471

Hours	Mon-Thurs: 4-12	Trains	Stoke Newington Rail
	Fri: 4-1		
	Sat: 12-1 Sun: 12-11	Buses	Routes 67, 73, 106,
			149, 243, 276
Online	@jollybutchers		Northwold Road
	jollybutchers.co.uk		

What to Drink
Anything by Dark Star, Thornbridge, Marble or (reasonably) local heroes Redemption

Food
Comfort food – from Bratwurst to Stroganoff to apple crumble

Unless you live nearby, Tube-less Stoke Newington can be a bit of a bugger to get to - which is a shame, since there's at least one excellent reason to make the long hike north: The Jolly Butchers. This large, extremely red, street-corner pub is among the best craft beer venues in the city and certainly one of the more relaxed. There are few pubs more suitable for a late-afternoon pint than the Butchers (warning: it only opens at 4pm in the week), especially when the sun is streaming in through the big windows on two sides of the building.

Inside, there's a sort of faux-worn feel: despite having only been open since 2010, it feels well-loved. That's as much down to the atmosphere as to the pre-used tables and chairs, the mixed wall adornments (from some slightly creepy Fornasetti wallpaper to the whitewashed brickwork) and the long, well-loaded bar. It's a really nice place, but not ostentatiously so. This is Stoke Newington, not High Street Kensington.

And anyway, it's a huge improvement on what was here before: a grubby, occasionally borderline-dangerous joint that was open until 3am but which you had to be fairly well-lubricated to consider entering. The beautification of The Jolly Butchers matches the rise of N16. There are some people, of course, who are a bit grumpy about it but it's certain that this place is doing rather better business now.

Not that everyone is always happy at the Butchers. On a visit about a year back, I found the barmaid who served me in a fearful grump. London was getting her down: too many people, she said, too much going on. I tried to alleviate her mood but failed miserably – but by the time I returned for a second pint, she'd been cheered up by the happy buzz that had built up in the pub.

Much of that happiness must be down to the beer on offer. Like a lot of the better London boozers, The Jolly Butchers regularly updates its twitter feed with what's on and it reads like a who's who of British craft brewing. From Yorkshire there's Magic Rock, from Derbyshire there's Thornbridge, from Essex there's Crouch Vale and from Manchester there's Marble. And that's before you even get onto London's representatives, which could include Redemption, Camden Town and Meantime. If you like beer at all, you will find something here to your taste.

It's a model that more Londoners deserve to enjoy, which is probably why the owners recently opened the Crown and Anchor in Brixton, which operates on similarly satisfying principles. One day, everyone in the capital will have access to this quality of local, which might make it difficult to motivate yourself for the trip across town to The Jolly Butchers. Given this place's undeniable charm, though, I'd guess plenty of people will still make that pilgrimage.

RAILWAY TAVERN

2 St Jude Street, Dalston N16 8JT

North

Hours	Mon-Sat: 12-11 Sun: 12-10.30	Trains	Dalston Kingsland Rail
		Buses	Routes 149, 243, 488, 67, 76, N76 - Dalston Kingsland Station
Online	@RailwayTavern		

What to Drink	Food
Kernel IPA	Thai

It doesn't take long to establish which railway is being celebrated here. There are pictures of the Tube (and a luggage rack) hanging on the walls and the fabric used to cover the seating looks suspiciously like it has been pilfered from a Northern Line carriage. Thankfully, the ambiance at the Railway Tavern Ale House is somewhat more relaxing than the average rush hour tube home.

London is a recurring theme throughout the pub so you'll find plenty of the capital's new breed of craft brewers on offer. Redemption - the Tottenham brewers whose beers effortlessly bridge the gap between old-school real ale and craft beer - are regulars on the hand pumps and you can expect to find The Kernel and Camden Town bottles in the fridge. However, on first glance, the food doesn't seem quite so London. It's Thai. Then again, in a city where more than three hundred languages are spoken, it would be a terrible shame if every pub sold pie and mash. And some of the modern London beers are probably more at home with a Thai green curry than they are paired with fish and chips.

One word of warning, however: there's another pub close to Dalston Kingsland Station that bears the same name. Make sure you don't alight there - this is the stop for craft beer.

DUKE'S BREW & QUE

33 Downham Road, De Beauvoir Town, Hackney N1 5AA
Tel: 020 3006 0795

North

Hours	Mon-Weds: 4-11	Trains	Haggerston
	Thurs: 4-11.30		Overground
	Fri: 4-12 Sat: 11-12		
	Sun: 11-11	Buses	Routes 67, 243, 149, 242
			Haggeston Station /
Online	@LoganBeaver		Downham Road
	dukesjoint.com		

| What to Drink | Food |
| Beavertown | Ribs and barbecue classics |

Americans are obsessed with barbecue. And when Americans talk about barbecue, they don't mean carbonised sausages and medium-rare chicken legs: they mean pulled pork and ribs. They're rhapsodising about cuts of meat that take seven days to cook at fifty degrees in an old oven out back that grandpa built during the Depression.

Londoners can now join in the barbecue love, courtesy of Logan Plant (son of Robert, whose band was even more popular than barbecue in the US during the 1970s) and his American business partner Byron Knight, the men behind Duke's. But Duke's is not just about barbecue: there's also excellent beer, which includes a variety of brews made on-site under the name Beavertown. You've got 8 Ball, a Rye IPA with balls, Neck Oil, a best bitter that pays homage to the beers of Logan's native Black Country, and Smog Rocket, a smoked porter. Even if it weren't for the food, it would be worth heading down to Duke's to enjoy the beer.

HOWL AT THE MOON

178 Hoxton Street N1 5LH
Tel: 020 3341 2525

North

Hours	Sun-Thurs: 12-11 Fri & Sat:12-1	Trains	Hoxton or Haggerston Overground
Online	@hoxtonhowl hoxtonhowl.com	Buses	Routes 67,149, 242, 243, 394 St. Leonard's Hospital

What to Drink	Food
Thornbridge Chiron	Bar snacks

It's nice to find a pub that caters for both craft beer converts and old-school drinkers. Visit Howl at the Moon on a Saturday afternoon and you'll find young shavers drinking BrewDog, Redemption and Thornbridge, while those who have seen it all down Hoxton way nurse more mainstream pints in the corner. And then there'll be the Australians, stumbling up to the bar and ordering 'a glass of the strongest spirit you've got' to go with their beer. You have to respect that.

You've also got to respect Hoxton Street, which still has a feel of the old East End. There's a pie and mash shop down the way (called F Cooke) where the floor is covered in sawdust in case the patrons spill their eels. Then there's The White Horse, which is one of two pubs in this part of town with that name. The other is an old-fashioned strip joint. If you're hoping to shove pound coins into a pint pot whilst a young woman takes her clothes off, you've gone the wrong way, but at least the beer is better.

But not as good as it is at Howl at the Moon. The range changes so regularly that there's no real point listing what you might find, but one thing is clear: everyone is welcome.

LISTINGS
OTHER NORTH CRAFT BEER DESTINATIONS

THE WENLOCK ARMS
26 Wenlock Road N1 7TA
Tel: 020 7608 3406
Online: wenlock-arms.co.uk
@thewenlock_arms
Mon: 4pm - 12am
Tues-Thurs & Sun: 12pm - 12am
Fri & Sat: 12pm - 1am

THE CHARLES LAMB
16 Elia Street, Islington N1 8DE
Tel: 020 7837 5040
Online: thecharleslambpub.com
@thecharleslamb
Mon & Tues: 4pm - 11pm
Weds-Sat: 12pm - 11pm
Sun: 12pm - 10.30pm

THE BARNSBURY
209 Liverpool Road, Islington N1 1LX
Tel: 020 7607 5519
Online: thebarnsbury.co.uk
@thebarnsburypub
Mon-Sun: 12pm - 11pm

THE EARL OF ESSEX

25 Danbury Street N1 8LE
Tel: 020 7424 5828
Online: earlofessex.net
@TheEarlofEssex1
Mon-Weds: 3pm - 11.30pm
Thurs: 12pm - 11.30pm
Fri & Sat: 12pm - 12.30am
Sun: 12pm - 11pm

WENLOCK & ESSEX

18-26 Essex Road, Islington N1 8LN
Tel: 020 7704 0871
Online: wenlockandessex.com
@wenlockandessex
Mon-Weds: 12pm - 11.30pm
Thu:12pm - 12am
Fri & Sat: 12pm - 2am
Sun: 12pm - 11.30pm

THE NORTH POLE

188 New North Road N1 7BJ
Tel: 020 7354 5400
Online: thenorthpolepub.co.uk
@thenorthpolepub
Mon-Thurs: 11am - 11pm
Fri & Sat: 11am - 12am
Sun: 11am - 10.30pm

THE PARCEL YARD

King's Cross Station, Euston Road N1 9AP
Tel: 020 7713 7258
Online: parcelyard.co.uk
@TheParcelYard
Mon-Sat: 8am - 11pm
Sun: 9am - 10.30pm

THE BULL

13 North Hill, Highgate N6 4AB
Tel: 020 8341 0510
Online: thebullhighgate.co.uk
@Bull_Highgate
Sun-Thurs: 12pm - 11.30pm
Fri & Sat: 12pm - 12am

THE DUKE OF HAMILTON

23 New End, Hampstead NW3 1JD
Tel: 020 7794 0258
Online: thedukeofhamilton.com
@dukeofhamilton
Mon-Sat: 11am - 11pm
Sun: 11am - 10.30pm

TAPPING THE ADMIRAL

77 Castle Road, Kentish Town NW1 8SU
Tel: 020 7267 6118
Online: tappingtheadmiral.co.uk
@tappingadmiral
Mon-Sat: 12pm - 11pm
Sun: 12pm - 10.30pm

THE SNOOTY FOX

75 Grosvenor Avenue N5 2NN
Tel: 020 7354 9532
Online: snootyfoxlondon.co.uk
@snootyfoxlondon
Mon-Thurs: 4pm - 11pm
Fri: 4pm - 1am
Sat: 12pm - 1am   **Sun:** 12pm - 10.30pm

THE LAMB

54 Holloway Road N7 8JL
Tel: 020 7619 9187
@thelambpub
Mon: 4pm - 11pm
Tues-Thurs: 4pm - 12am
Fri: 4pm - 1am
Sat: 12pm - 1am
Sun: 12pm - 11pm

East

THE FOX

372 Kingsland Road E8 4DA
Tel: 07807 217734

Hours	Mon-Thurs: 12-1 Fri-Sun: 12-3	Trains	Haggerston Overground
Online	@thefoxe8 thefoxe8.com	Buses	Routes 67, 149, 242, 243 Haggerston Station

What to Drink
Thornbridge Chiron

Food
Good pub snacks – cheese, pork belly – plus more substantial meals

You might expect to find a jukebox, a darts board or a pool table at your local pub, but a photo booth? Not really. Still, quirkiness is to be encouraged (within reason) and the photo booth at The Fox has no doubt taken a few interesting pictures in its time. A few of the participants probably regretted it the next day, too.

Not many of those who have crossed the threshold here will regret it, however. It's a huge, street-corner boozer that commands a long stretch of the Kingsland Road and the more eagle-eyed craft beer fan will have spotted the likes of Thornbridge, Dark Star, Harviestoun and Oakham long before he makes it to the bar. There's also a rooftop terrace where, whilst soaking up some sunshine, you might reflect that Kingsland Road forms part of one of the oldest thoroughfares in England. Ermine Street, which once ran from London to York, was almost certainly lined with places to quench your thirst back then – although, lacking a photo booth, Roman drinkers weren't able to preserve the moment for posterity.

SEBRIGHT ARMS

31-35 Coate Street E2 9AG
Tel: 020 7729 0937

Hours	Mon-Weds: 5-11 Thurs-Sat: 5-12 Sun: 12-10.30	Trains	Cambridge Heath Overground
Online	@sebrightarms sebrightarms.co.uk	Buses	Routes 48, 55, 106, 254 Cambridge Heath Station

What to Drink	Food
Camden Town, Meantime, London Fields	Burgers

Let's be honest: this can be an intimidating place. Not only is it a fairly forbidding-looking structure - more gangster's hide-out than cosy hostelry - but the denizens of this large East London pub are at the very vanguard of all things hip. Many a strong man's stomach has done a loop-the-loop at the thought of wandering in here ill-coiffured for the occasion.

Of course, the reality is quite different. Despite its reputation as one of London's more fashionable drinking dens, it's a very welcoming place with a surprisingly old-fashioned feel. This looks like an old-school pub, but it differs in one key aspect: the quality of the beer. At many of East London's remaining spit-and-sawdust boozers, the beer runs the gamut from Carling to Carlsberg but things are a lot more varied here. The Sebright is a music venue, too, and the current home of Lucky Chip, one of the capital's most well-regarded burger-flipping operations. If you're tempted to give the Sebright a swerve you need only know that your bravery will be richly rewarded.

THE COCK TAVERN

315 Mare Street E8 1EJ

East

Hours	Mon-Sat: 12-1 Sun: 12-10.30	**Trains**	Hackney Central Overground
Online	@TheCockTavernE8 thecocktavern.co.uk	**Buses**	Routes 30, 38, 48, 55, 106, 236 Dalston Kingsland

What to Drink
Howling Hops – the beer made on site

Food
Pork pies, pickled stuff

There's been much talk of late about the cost of a glass of beer. There are plenty of good reasons why craft beer, made as it is on a small scale using the best ingredients, might be more expensive than your average lager but its nonetheless an unpleasant surprise when a round of four drinks doesn't leave a great deal of change from £20.

It's this situation that makes The Cock Tavern's stance on beer prices all the more welcome. Cask ales at this handsome old-school Hackney pub (where the interior, all dark wood, handpumps and jars of pickled items, is as old-school as the prices) are generally less than £3.50 a pint – and when you consider that you can expect to find the likes of Magic Rock, Red Willow and Redemption on the bar, that's very decent by London standards. The Cock Tavern is brought to you by the people behind The Southampton Arms, so there are high hopes for Howling Hops, the on-site microbrewery.

THE COCK
TAVERN

LOTS OF
NICE
BEER
&
LOVELY
MEAT

TAP EAST

7 International Square, Westfield, Stratford City E20 1EE
Tel: 020 8555 4467

Hours	Mon-Sat: 11-11	Trains	Stratford
	Sun: 12-10	Buses	Routes 25, 69, 86, 97,
Online	@tapeast		104, 108 - Stratford

What to Drink
Coffee in the Morning - a stout brewed using El Salvadorian coffee beans

Food
Cheese, pies, sandwiches

This summer's Olympic Games necessitated the construction of a stadium, a velodrome, a swimming pool and a shopping centre on a piece of derelict land in Stratford. A shopping centre you ask? Welcome to London. The good news, however, is that said shopping centre is home to Tap East, a bar and micro-brewery set up by the good folk from beer merchants Utobeer. Given that Heineken had snaffled the rights to sell beer in the Olympic Park, Tap East came as tremendous news: you could go to the Games (if you got tickets) and drink decent beer.

Tap East - all glass, tiling and high tables - is pretty much right at the back of Westfield Stratford as you approach from the tube, and it's an interesting if over-long journey. For a start, things gradually get more expensive as you progress through this cavernous temple to stuff. McDonald's becomes a shop selling acorn-fed Iberico ham; Greggs becomes a Japanese supermarket. Similarly, Tap East could never be described as cheap, but at least you'll get something worthwhile for your cash – unlike in the Olympic Stadium.

THE RED LION

640 High Road, Leytonstone E11 3AA
Tel: 020 8988 2929

East

Hours	Mon-Weds: 12-11	Trains	Leytonstone
	Thurs: 12-12		Overground
	Fri & Sat: 12-2 Sun: 12-11		
		Buses	66, 145, 257, N8,
Online	@ red_lion_e11		W13, W14
	theredlionleytonstone.com		Kirkdale Road

What to Drink
Magic Rock

Food
Simple but elegant: sea bream, perhaps, or a lamb chop

Few tourists make it out this far East; in all honesty, few Londoners do either. This is a real shame. The Red Lion stands comparison with any pub in the city, and that's in terms of beer, food and atmosphere: the holy trinity of the pub experience, as Alan Partridge might put it.

On the bar (cask and keg) you might expect to find the likes of BrewDog, Thornbridge, Magic Rock and Dark Star and there's plenty more in the fridge, too. The beer selection is probably more imaginative and well-considered than at any pub that, like The Red Lion, finds itself out in the wilds of London Transport's Zone 4. Not only is the beer excellent but the food - from bar snacks like Scotch eggs up to more substantial gastro-style main meals - should keep even the most particular of patrons satisfied.

All of this would be less impressive if The Red Lion didn't feel so welcoming. Ace beer writer Mark Dredge described it as a "modern local", and that sounds right. It's got the beer to attract drinkers from all over London and the charm and warmth to ensure locals feel valued. Indeed, given the quality of The Red Lion, it might convince more than a few of those beer lovers to make Leytonstone their new home.

BRODIE'S BREWERY

816A High Road, Leyton E10 6AE
www.brodiesbeers.co.uk

CRAFT BEER
BREWERY

Hours	Look out for
By appointment only	Dalston Black IPA

There can't be many brewers around who make as many different beers as Brodie's. One well-respected American website lists in the region of one hundred and fifty, which is not bad going when you consider the brewery was only founded in 2008. Some of these beers are pretty unusual, too, at least for the British market – like their IPA made with Brettanomyces, a yeast whose presence creates the sort of sour flavours much coveted by in-the-know beer lovers.

Brodie's expansive approach has not gone unnoticed. Mikkel Borg Bjergso, the man behind well-regarded Danish brewery Mikkeller, came to London earlier this year to brew a beer with Brodie's, for example. But there's a down-to-earth quality to Brodie's too: their brewery tap, The King William IV in Leyton, couldn't be more old-school if it tried. The beers are cheap (and plentiful) and food is of the basic-but-filling variety. You don't have to go to Leyton to drink Brodie's, though, although it's worth the trip. Two central London pubs – The Old Coffee House in Soho and The Cross Keys in Covent Garden – serve their beer and they now send bottles around the country. Even given that, though, you're unlikely to ever try them all.

LISTINGS

OTHER EAST CRAFT BEER DESTINATIONS

STRONGROOM BAR & KITCHEN
120-124 Curtain Road, Shoreditch EC2A 3SQ
Tel: 020 7426 5103
Online: strongroombar.com
@strongroombar
Mon: 9am - 11pm
Tue-Weds: 9am - 12am
Thurs: 9am - 1am
Fri: 9am - 2am
Sat: 12pm - 2am
Sun: 12pm - 10pm

THE WHITE HORSE
153, Hoxton Street N1 6PJ
Tel: 020 7729 8512
Online: hoxtonwhitehorse.com
@HoxWhiteHorse
Mon-Weds : 12pm - 11pm
Thurs: 12pm - 12am
Fri & Sat: 12pm - 1.30am
Sun: 12pm - 12am

BREWDOG - SHOREDITCH (NEW)
51-55 Bethnal Green Road E1 6LA
Tel: 020 77499670
Online: brewdog.com
@brewdog
Hours TBC

THE CARPENTERS' ARMS
73 Cheshire Street E2 6EG
Tel: 020 7739 6342
Online: carpentersarmsfreehouse.com
Mon, Tues, Weds: 4pm -11.30pm
Thurs & Sun: 12pm -11.30pm
Fri & Sat: 12pm - 12.30am

REDCHURCH BREWERY
273 Poyser Street E2 9RF
Tel: 07968 173 097
Online: theredchurchbrewery.com
@redchurchbrewer
Look out for: Great Eastern IPA

THE FLORIST ARMS
255 Globe Road, Bethnal Green E2 0JD
Tel: 020 8981 1100
Online: thefloristarms.co.uk
Mon - Sat: 11am - 11pm
Sun: 12pm - 10.30pm

THE CAMEL
277 Globe Road, Bethnal Green E2 0JD
Tel: 020 8983 9888
Online: thecamele2.co.uk
@thecamelpub
Mon - Sun: 12pm -11pm

THE DOVE

24-28 Broadway Market E8 4QJ
Tel: 020 7275 7617
Online: dovepubs.com
@DovePubs
Mon-Fri: 12pm -11pm
Sat & Sun: 12pm -12pm

LONDON FIELDS BREWERY

365-366 Warburton Street E8 3RR
Tel: 020 7254 7174
Online: londonfieldsbrewery.co.uk
@LdnFldsBrewery
Look out for: Hackney Hopster

CRATE

Queen's Yard, Hackney Wick E9 5EN
Tel: 07834 275 687
Online: cratebrewery.com
@CrateBrewery
Mon-Sun: 12pm -11pm

THREE COMPASSES

99 Dalston Lane E8 1NH
Tel: 07779 003 327
Online: 3compasses.blogspot.co.uk
@3compasses
Mon-Fri: 4pm -11pm   **Sat & Sun:** 11am - 11pm

PEMBURY TAVERN

90 Amhurst Road, Hackney E8 1JH
Tel: 020 8986 8597
Online: individualpubs.co.uk/pembury
@PemburyTavern
Mon-Sun: 12pm -11pm

DUKE OF WELLINGTON

119 Balls Pond Road N1 4BL
Tel: 020 7275 7640
Online: thedukeofwellingtonn1.com
@TheDukeN1
Mon-Weds: 3pm - 12am
Thurs & Fri: 3pm - 1am
Sat: 12pm - 1am
Sun: 12pm -11.30pm

THE CLAPTON HART

231 Lower Clapton Road E5 8EG
Tel: 020 8985 8124
Online: claptonhart.com
@claptonhart
Mon -Thurs: 4pm - 11pm
Fri: 4pm - 12am
Sat: 12pm - 12am
Sun: 12pm -11pm

EAST LONDON BREWING COMPANY

Unit 45, Fairways Business Centre, Lammas Road
E10 7QB
Tel: 020 8539 0805
Online: eastlondonbrewing.com
@eastlondonbrew
Look out for: ELB Pale Ale

KING WILLIAM IV

816 High Road, Leyton E10 6AE
Tel: 020 8556 2460
Online: brodiesbeers.co.uk
@BrodiesBeers
Mon-Thurs: 11am - 12am
Fri & Sat: 11am - 1am
Sun: 12am - 12pm

South/
South East

THE DEAN SWIFT

10 Gainsford Street, Butler's Wharf SE1 2NE
Tel: 020 7357 0748

Hours	Sun-Thurs: 12-12 Fri & Sat: 12-1	Trains	London Bridge Overground / Tower Bridge Tube
Online	@deanswiftse1 thedeanswift.com	Buses	Routes 47, 188, 343, 381, N47, N381 - Tower Bridge Police Station

What to Drink	Food
Dean Swift Pilsner or The Kernel	Everything from pasta to salads via burgers

This is London's beer district, or at least it was. Once upon a time, many of the breweries that made the city famous – such as Courage and Barclay Perkins – were based along the south side of the river. Those days are long gone, of course, but you can still just about smell malt on the Bermondsey air, and not just because The Kernel's brewery is so close. The Dean Swift is also keeping the spirit of good beer alive in this part of town.

It's a cosy little place – estate agents might call it bijou - but that's no reason to dislike it. On the contrary, there are plenty of reasons to appreciate this spot: it's a hidden beer oasis just a short stroll from the Tower of London, for a start. Those bored of beefeaters can escape for a beer and perhaps even some beef - the food here is as well-regarded as the beer.

Dean Swift, it must be assumed, is named for the great Anglo-Irish satirist Jonathan Swift, who had his own views on drinking. "Better belly burst than good liquor be lost," he once quipped. We can all drink to that.

THE RAKE

14 Winchester Walk SE1 9AG
Tel: 020 7407 0557

Hours	Mon-Fri: 12-11	Trains	London Bridge
	Sat: 10-11		Tube & Overground
	Sun: 12-8		
		Buses	Routes 47, 343, 381,
Online	@rakebar		N47, N381 - London
	utobeer.co.uk/		Bridge Station
	aboutus_rake.html		

What to Drink
Take your pick: it's all good

Food
Crisps and bar snacks

How important is The Rake? One of the brewers who has scribbled on the walls of this tiny Borough boozer is in no doubt: 'The Marquee of beer', is how Jeff Rosenmeier of Henley's world-beating Lovibonds describes it, putting it on the same level as the legendary Wardour Street club where so many of Britain's most famous rock stars got their start. He might have a point. The Rake opened in 2006, well before most London pubs noticed craft beer existed, and has punched consistently above its flyweight status (try swinging a cat in here) ever since.

Its potency is thanks in no small part to the fact that it is owned by Utobeer - the beer wholesalers who run an extremely popular stall in Borough Market and therefore have access to a mind-blowing variety of beer. As a result, the offerings change so regularly here that it's almost a surprise to see something you've had before.

There are regular festivals, showcasing beers from different parts of the UK, and 'brewery takeovers' are not uncommon, too: Welsh tyros Little Rebel Brewing Company recently took control of the bar, for example.

It's on busy days at the market that The Rake really comes into its own though. Inspecting stalls bursting to the brim with organic, free-range, cured-on-a-Cantabrian-virgin's-knee Chorizo and not-so-keenly-priced Dover Sole is tiring and thirsty stuff. This makes The Rake something of a Godsend, especially when it's warm enough to sit in the yard alongside (which is three or four Saturdays a year, at least).

But if you are forced inside by London's weather, then there's plenty to entertain you. The walls are covered with stickers, pump clips (the brewer's branding that goes on the front of beer pumps) and then there are the scribbles like Rosenmeier's. It's hard to escape the conclusion that anyone who's anyone in the world of craft beer has dropped in at some point. 'Beer Speaks, People Mumble,' is what Ron from Californian hop-lovers Lagunitas has written. They certainly do, Ron, especially when the beer's this tasty.

Borough – as befits a place where food and drink is taken seriously - boasts a few places with pretensions of being beer shrines. There's The Market Porter, which lost a lot of its charm if not its custom after a refit a few years back, and Brew Wharf, which finally looks to be getting its act together even if prices remain sometimes eye-wateringly high. Despite being the titchiest of the lot, though, The Rake has the biggest claim on that title. Small is beautiful.

THE KERNEL BREWERY

Arch 11, Dockley Road Industrial Estate SE16 3SF
www.thekernelbrewery.com

Hours
Sat: 9-3, or by appointment

Look out for
Export Stout 1890 London

There's something hidden away at The Kernel's home in Bermondsey that tells you all you need to know about the brewery: a motley collection of old barrels. Four of them have been used to house whisky, four once contained Burgundy. Now they're being pressed into service to age Kernel beer, and the results are likely to be worth looking out for. Why? Because pretty much everything The Kernel have done so far has been impressive. It's no exaggeration to suggest that this is the most highly-rated brewery in the city, which is remarkable when you consider how it all started. Evin O'Riordain, the man who created The Kernel, was a home brewer inspired to make bold-flavoured beers by a spell in New York, where he had gone to teach the locals about cheese (he used to work for Neal's Yard Dairy, London's premier British cheesemonger). He had no brewing training and a lot of his knowledge, he readily admits, came from the internet. Now he and his team are making some remarkable, world-beating beers.

The beers The Kernel are most famous for fit into two stables: New-World-hopped pale ales and IPAS, and old, dark London classics like porter and stout. In the second category, the Export Stout 1890 London is particularly worth seeking out, especially for those that love coffee. Any number of stouts are described as being 'coffee-like', but few come close to the pure espresso hit you get from this beer, although there is more to it than that - it's also complex and rewarding.

However that's not all The Kernel make, as the barrels demonstrate. Their Saison - a tribute to the crisp, refreshing traditional beers of French-speaking Belgium - is always worth tracking down. Their recent move from a previous site on nearby Rope Walk, to a larger brewery some five hundred metres south-eastwards, has also given them more scope to experiment.

Gratifyingly, both the current and previous breweries are housed in the arches under the railway that leads out of London Bridge. This is a suitably down-to-earth venue for a brewery that aims to bring great beer to ordinary Londoners, a mission they have tackled with some success. The new brewery means that kegged Kernel beer is starting to crop up all over London which, given the popularity and resulting clamour for their bottled beers, gives more of us a chance to get our hands on some. Getting down to the brewery on Saturday mornings when it is opened up to sell beer, is still your best way to stock up and ensure you get to sample their latest experiments. If you're lucky, you might even get a glimpse of those barrels.

THE KERNEL BREWERY LONDON

INDIA PALE ALE

BLACK VI

6.3% ABV

STORMBIRD

25 Camberwell Church Street SE5 8TR
Tel: 020 7708 4460

Hours	Sun-Thurs: 12-12 Fri & Sat: 12-1	Trains	Denmark Hill Overground
Online	@ stormbirdse5 thestormbirdpub.co.uk	Buses	Routes 12, 36, 171, 345, 436, N89 - Camberwell Church Street

What to Drink	Food
Redemption, Brodie's, Dark Star	N/A

Stormbird took a while to get into its stride. At first, it seemed almost nervous to announce it had arrived, scared perhaps of offending its older brother, The Hermit's Cave, which can be found across Camberwell Church Street. It can still be mystifyingly unpopulated but the word is finally getting out - Camberwell boasts one of the best craft beer pubs around. It also has some of the friendliest staff, who are only too happy to guide you through the mystifying variety of beer on offer. The fridges are full of unexpected delights, which might include the magnificent Stone Cali-Belgique IPA and Deus - Belgian beer's answer to Champagne.

It's a satisfyingly old-school space, for all the shiny, colourful beer taps on the bar: a rectangular room, wooden tables and a handful of handpumps. You could almost forget that until recently this place was called the Funky Munky. Truth be told, it didn't live up to its moniker often enough to survive and Stormbird's more reserved approach is already proving more successful. They've certainly got the clientele, what with Camberwell College of Arts just down the road towards Peckham - now there's somewhere crying out for a proper craft beer den.

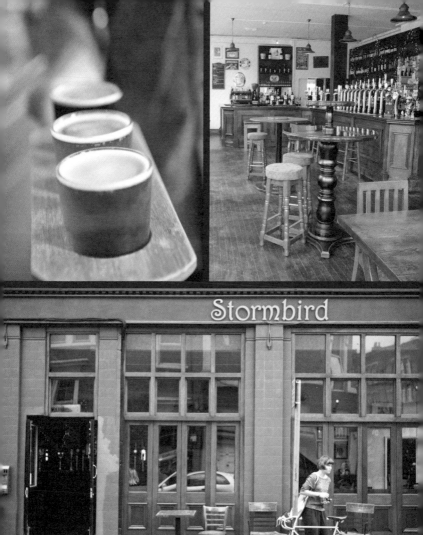

GREENWICH UNION

56 Royal Hill, Greenwich SE10 8RT
Tel: 020 8692 6258

Hours	Mon-Fri: 12-11	Trains	Greenwich Rail
	Sat: 11-11		& DLR
	Sun: 11.30-10.30		
		Buses	Routes 180,199, 386
Online	greenwichunion.com		Greenwich Station

What to Drink
Anything by Meantime

Food
Classic pub food:
burgers, pies, fish and chips,
sandwiches

Plenty of tourists make the trek out to Greenwich. They walk around the Royal Naval College, gawp at the restored Cutty Sark, admire the magnificent Royal Observatory and then, more often than not, they go for a drink at one of the pubs along the river, like the Trafalgar Tavern. There's nothing wrong with that - it's a magnificent structure - but if you're in search of great beer, head up the hill towards the Greenwich Union, the first pub opened by local heroes Meantime.

As you'd expect, Meantime's beer dominates the bar. The Greenwich brewers' offerings are aimed directly at the man on the Clapham Omnibus: far more flavourful than your average pub offering but nonetheless truly accessible. If that doesn't satisfy you, then there's plenty of beer from elsewhere, too – and bottles can now be taken away. Not that you're likely to be in any rush to leave.

MEANTIME BREWING CO.

Blackwall Lane SE10 0AR
www.meantimebrewing.com

Hours	Brewery tours by appointment	Look out for	Meantime IPA

The year 2000 seems a long time ago. That was when Alastair Hook launched Meantime, and what a revolutionary decision it was, at least in retrospect. Meantime started by brewing a Vienna Lager called Union. Then they put it in kegs. Quality lager in kegs: not very British, but then Hook's approach never has been.

Inspired by German tradition and American innovation, Hook set out to remind Britons of the brewing heritage they had squandered. This means that, for all Hook's dismay at what has happened to British brewing since the war, there are few more faithful renditions than Meantime's excellent versions of those London classics - Porter and India Pale Ale. Meantime has expanded a lot over the past few years and, thanks to a new brewery, you can find their beers – in particular, London Lager and London Pale Ale – across the city. The best place for a Meantime, though, remains in Greenwich, perhaps at the Greenwich Union pub or the Old Brewery. There is nowhere better to mull over both how London beer has changed in the last twelve years, and how it continues to evolve.

CATFORD BRIDGE TAVERN

Station Approach, Catford Bridge SE6 4RE
Tel: 020 3066 2060

Hours	Mon-Thurs: 4-12	Trains	Catford & Catford
	Fri: 4-1		Bridge Overground
	Sat: 12-1		
	Sun: 12-12	Buses	Routes 160, 320,
Online	@catfordtavern		336 - Catford
	catfordbridgetavern.com		Bridge Station

What to Drink
Magic Rock

Food
Gastropub grub and high-quality bar snacks

People can be terribly mean about Catford. True, it's not glamorous and the shopping options are a little dispiriting, but this part of south-east London has at least two things going for it. One is a giant fibreglass sculpture of a cat outside the shopping centre. The second and most important draw is the Catford Bridge Tavern, which would be far better known if it were in a more fashionable part of town.

The Catford Bridge Tavern was formerly known as The Copperfield, as depressing a station pub as you could find. That was until earlier this year when the pub's fortunes were revived by Antic, the company currently busy transforming boozers all over London, who installed enough decent ale and craft beer to satisfy the most fastidious of drinkers. Interestingly, they also sought to help revive another traditional pub staple by installing a bar billiards table. The Catford Bridge Tavern loses points for its table being up against a wall that makes it hard for southpaws to play, but we'll let them off as long as they keep serving great beer.

LISTINGS

DRAFT HOUSE – TOWER BRIDGE
206 – 208 Tower Bridge Road SE1 2UP
Tel: 020 7378 9995
Online: drafthouse.co.uk
@drafthouseuk
Mon-Sat: 12pm - 11pm
Sun: 12pm - 10.30pm

THE CROWN
108 Blackfriars Road SE1 8HW
Tel: 020 7261 9524
Online: the-crown-london.co.uk
Mon-Thurs & Sat: 12pm - 11pm
Fri: 12pm - 12am
Sun: 12pm - 10.30pm

SIMON THE TANNER
231 Long Lane SE1 4PR
Tel: 020 7357 8740
Online: simonthetanner.co.uk
@Simon_theTanner
Mon-Sat: 12pm - 11pm
Sun: 12pm - 10.30pm

THE DOG & BELL
116 Prince Street, Deptford SE8 3JD
Tel: 020 8692 5664
Online: thedogandbell.co.uk
Mon-Sun: 12pm - 11.30pm

THE ROYAL ALBERT
460 New Cross Road, New Cross SE14 6TJ
Tel: 020 8692 3737
Online: royalalbertpub.com
@theroyalalbert
Mon- Thurs: 4pm -12am
Fri: 4pm - 2am
Sat: 12pm - 1am
Sun: 12pm - 12am

THE OLD NUN'S HEAD
15 Nunhead Green SE15 3QQ
Tel: 020 7639 4007
Online: theoldnunshead.co.uk
@theoldnunshead
Mon-Thurs: 12pm - 12am
Fri & Sat: 12pm - 1am
Sun: 12pm - 11.30pm

EAST DULWICH TAVERN
1 Lordship Lane SE22 8EW
Tel: 020 8693 1316
Online: eastdulwichtavern.com
@edtse22
Mon-Thurs: 12pm - 12am
Fri & Sat: 12pm - 1am
Sun: 12pm - 12am

DRAFT HOUSE – LORDSHIP

21 Lordship Lane SE22 8EW
Tel: 020 8299 3511
Online: drafthouse.co.uk
@DraftHouseUK
Mon-Fri: 12pm -11pm
Sat & Sun: 12pm - Late

THE FLORENCE

131 - 133 Dulwich Road, Herne Hill SE24 ONG
Tel: 020 7326 4987
Online: florencehernehill.com
@theflorencepub
Mon-Thurs: 11.30am - 12am
Fri: 11.30am - 1am
Sat: 11am - 1am
Sun: 11am - 12am

THE RAVENSBOURNE ARMS

323 Lewisham High Street SE13 6NR
Tel: 020 8613 7070
Online: ravensbournearms.com
@RavensbourneArm
Mon-Thurs: 12pm - 11pm
Fri & Sat: 12pm - 1am
Sun: 12pm - 11pm

BLYTHE HILL TAVERN

319 Stanstead Road, Catford SE23 1JB
Tel: 020 8690 5176
Online: N/A
Mon-Wed: 11am - 11pm
Thurs-Sat: 11am - 12am
Sun: 12pm - 11pm

THE SYLVAN POST

24 – 28 Dartmouth Road, Forest Hill SE23 3XU
Tel: 020 8291 5712
Online: sylvanpost.com
@SylvanPost
Mon-Fri: 4pm - 12am
Sat & Sun: 12pm - 12am

THE GRAPE AND GRAIN

2 Anerley Hill, Crystal Palace SE19 2AA
Tel: 020 8778 4109
Online: thegrapeandgrainse19.co.uk
@TheGrapeandGrain
Mon-Thurs: 12pm - 11pm
Fri & Sat: 12pm - 1am
Sun: 12pm - 10.30pm

WESTOW HOUSE

79 Westow Hill SE19 1TX
Tel: 020 8670 0654
Online: westowhouse.com
@westow_house
Mon-Thurs: 12pm - 12am
Fri & Sat: 12pm - 2am
Sun: 12pm - 11pm

West /
South West

CASK

6 Charlwood Street, Pimlico SW1V 6EE
Tel: 020 7630 7225

Hours	Mon-Sat: 12-11 Sun: 12-10.30	Trains	Pimlico Underground
Online	@CASK_PUB_SW1 caskpubandkitchen.com	Buses	Routes 24, 360, C10 - Pimlico Academy

What to Drink
Thornbridge, Mikkeller, De Molen

Food
Burgers, steak, fish and chips – the classics

Before Cask opened in 2009, it was surprisingly difficult to find certain breweries' products in the capital. Take Thornbridge, for example: London sightings of their hugely respected ales, like Jaipur and Kipling, were as rare as cheap trips in a black cab. Cask changed that. From the start they've had a close relationship with Thornbridge, and Dark Star for that matter, and drinking in London has been much the better for it.

For all that, Cask is not a very promising sight. It won't win any architectural awards - squeezed under a large and unsightly 1970s block of flats, it only begins to impress once you are inside. In terms of variety, there are perhaps two or three pubs in the capital that can compare (and one of them is sister venue Craft Beer Company). This is a place where, if you have the money, you can drink your way around the world.

Any decent trip around the world, of course, requires a map (or perhaps an app) and Cask has its own version in the form of a huge beer list. The first time I had a flick through this gargantuan document, I became so engrossed that when the barman returned to take my order I hadn't decided. How can you decide with so many great options? Cask regulars know all about the tyranny of choice.

They know plenty about beer, too, even if Cask is situated a long way from craft beer's London stronghold in the East. Cask attracts an interesting and varied crowd, with any number of beer-loving civil servants (many of them desperately checking their watches to ensure they can get another drink in and still make the 19.34 to Sevenoaks) due to the government departments that are based nearby.

There are plenty of hardcore beer-lovers, too, of course, and Cask does its best to ensure they continue to make the trip to Pimlico. There are regular 'Meet the Brewer' nights, when a brewery takes over the bar to showcase their latest offerings, where past events have seen brewers from Mallinsons, Red Willow and Revolutions fielding questions and getting to meet their adoring public. The reality is that many of the best new brewers are beer lovers with a talent for making it: craft beer is punk by another name, even if some of the more experimental beers might strike Sid Vicious and Co. as a little too prog-rock.

Not that Cask has offended quite as many people as punk. The opposite, in fact: the amount of awards this pub has garnered demonstrates how it appeals to beer drinkers across the entire spectrum, from CAMRA to Beer Advocate, an American craft-beer focused website. London drinkers appreciate Cask, and so they should.

THE DRAFT HOUSE

74-76 Battersea Bridge Road SW11 3AG
Tel: 020 7228 6482

Hours	Mon-Fri: 12-11 Sat: 10-11 Sun: 10-10.30	Trains	Clapham Junction
		Buses	Routes 19, 49, 319, 345, N19, N31 Parkgate Road
Online	@DraftHouseWB drafthouse.co.uk		

What to Drink
Sambrook's Wandle

Food
Burgers, steaks – lots of meat

Charlie McVeigh is a driven man. He wants the world to know that beer is as good (if not better) with proper food as wine, and his chosen vehicle to convey this message is The Draft House. There are five Draft Houses in London now (the first central London venue – on the corner of Goodge and Charlotte Streets - being the most recent addition), so it seems like the message is getting through.

This, though, is where it all started. The Draft Houses differ here and there but essentially the theme is the same: excellent beer and hearty food. The hamburgers, in particular, are worth looking out for. They come in three varieties: The Smoke, The Yolk and, ahem, The Poke. The former is perhaps the best, not least because it has bacon on it and, as most gourmets know, there are few dishes that can't be improved with bacon.

The astute reader might have noticed that this is probably not the place for you if you're a vegetarian. Other items of note on the menu include a foot-long pork scratching (in case you feel in need of a coronary) and something called The Meat Bomb, which is a cross between a Scotch egg and Arancini. Even the snappily-named 'Hanoi Jane's Vietnam Salad' can be served with slow-roast pork belly and crackling for a small additional fee.

This passion for meat is matched by a love of beer. Draft House Westbridge has a particularly close relationship with local brewers Sambrook's and this is where the first pint of Wandle, their flagship ale, was served. But beer doesn't have to be local to make it into The Draft House: from South Australia (Cooper's) to Colorado (Left Hand), most of the beer world is represented here. If you were being particularly critical, you might accuse the beer selection of being a little conservative but it would be a strange beer lover who couldn't find plenty worth drinking.

It would also be a strange person who didn't enjoy the convivial atmosphere at The Draft House, too. Unlike many of the new breed of beer joints, The Draft House feels like a restaurant: this is not really the place to come just for a drink, although you can, of course. McVeigh – a charismatic, entertaining Old Etonian – has constructed a particularly West London-style ale house, where food is as important as beer.

Some people, of course, prefer wine as a companion to food. Charlie tackled that world-view during a series of dinners entitled 'Extreme Grape vs Grain' at The Draft House Tower Bridge earlier this year, which pitched his beer picks against a pal's wine choices in a series of four contests. Those who refuse to acknowledge beer's growing sophistication are going to have to get used to being told off, it seems.

POWDER KEG DIPLOMACY

147 St John's Hill SW11 1TQ
Tel: 020 7450 6457

Hours	Tue-Fri: 12-12	Trains	Clapham Junction
	Sat & Sun: 10-12		
		Buses	37, 39, 87, 156,
Online	@BaronPowderKeg		170, 337
	powderkegdiplomacy.co.uk		Brussels Road

What to Drink
Marble Lagonda IPA

Food
From decadent (a three-bird roast) to down-to-earth

Craft beer places don't generally feel the need for a theme but it seems you require more than just great beer to stand out in bar-heavy Clapham. Thus, Powder Keg Diplomacy is a colonial-era-accented beer venue, complete with pith helmet lampshades and other antique details. A lot of thought has obviously gone into making this place a bit different, and not only in terms of the décor. One interesting feature on the beer menu is the 'after-dinner' beer section: Powder Keg Diplomacy have cleverly noticed that many beers – like Magic Rock's Bearded Lady stout – are best enjoyed at leisure. Like a fine Brandy, except you get more for your cash.

It's this sort of cleverness that sets Powder Keg Diplomacy apart. The wine list, for example, is as impressive as the beer selection. This being sunny Clapham, there's also cocktails and fancy food with prices that reflect the Westside nature of this pub, so if you blanch at anything more expensive than a Happy Meal, this probably isn't the place for you. Those who don't mind paying for quality should go west to the Powder Keg. Safari gear not obligatory.

THE WHITE HORSE

1-3 Parsons Green SW6 4UL
Tel: 020 7736 2115

Hours	Sun-Weds: 9.30-11.30 Thurs-Sat: 9.30-12	Trains	Parsons Green
		Buses	Routes 22, N22 Parsons Green
Online	@whitehorsesw6 whitehorsesw6.com		

What to Drink
Try the Oakham JHB, or a tall
glass of Schneider Weisse

Food
'Modern British', they call it –
i.e. sophisticated pub grub

efore there was craft beer, there was The White Horse. Sometimes it can be easy for craft beer's more committed followers to forget that there was good drinking in England before the American-inspired revolution of the past ten years, but anyone acquainted with this magnificent Victorian pub will know better. The beer here has been excellent since the 1990s, when Mark Dorber – who has since decamped to the countryside – made the place famous for its dry-hopped Bass and its Belgian beers.

But while Mark has gone and the dry-hopped Bass is but a memory, the Belgian beers, and plenty more besides, are still here. You can expect to find perfectly-kept cask ale - including Oakham JHB, a citrusy golden ale that predates the current spate of similar beers - an interesting keg selection and bottles from around the world. There is something for everyone, including those who spend their lives seeking out the new and novel; The White Horse's selection is frequently refreshed and always refreshing.

This desire to bring regulars new drinking experiences finds another outlet in the regular beer festivals The White Horse puts on. Most notable, perhaps, is the American Beer Festival that takes place (appropriately enough) in July. Since 2008, when the pub delivered its first celebration of American beer, offerings from Sierra Nevada, Rogue, The Great Divide and many others have crossed the pond to reach the 'Sloaney Pony' - the nickname The White Horse acquired during the 1980s, when Fulham's upwardly mobile residents began to flock to the pub.

In fact, July is a great time to visit The White Horse since, given the vagaries of the British weather, it's one of the few months of the year when you can really make proper use of the big beer garden that faces onto Parsons Green. It's a genuinely relaxing spot for a drink if it's sunny but if it isn't, no need to panic: drinking inside The White Horse has its charms, too. The long tables, open fire, deep comfy armchairs and beer-memorabilia-festooned walls make this place feel like half pub, half gentleman's club.

The White Horse's menu, however, is not long on the boarding-school-style grub so beloved of some of London's more traditional members' clubs. The pub that took beer seriously years before anywhere else is still the place to go to if you're interested in pairing good grub with great beer. Not only does The White Horse regularly put on beer dinners – BrewDog were guests back in June – but the menu includes beer recommendations for each dish. Eat, drink and be very merry.

CROWN & ANCHOR

246 Brixton Road SW9 6AQ
Tel: 020 7737 7915

Hours	Mon-Thurs: 4.30-12	Trains	Brixton /
	Fri: 4.30-1		Stockwell Tube
	Sat: 12-1		
	Sun: 12-11	Buses	Routes 3, 59,
			133, 159, 415, N3
Online	@crownanchorsw9		Loughborough Rd.
	crownandanchorbrixton.co.uk		

What to Drink	Food
Ales change regularly but look out for	Pub classics
Dark Star	

There's plenty of great stuff in Brixton: some of the best street food around, a number of excellent drinking establishments, The Academy and a wide variety of interesting characters. But what Brixton lacked until very recently was somewhere that sold a decent range of excellent beer. No more. The Crown and Anchor has since filled that particular gap in Brixton's resume.

The Crown and Anchor looks pretty good, even before you consider the great beers on offer. The room itself is an impressive sight, all exposed brickwork and big windows. A huge bar runs down the wall and outside the pub's illuminated sign winks at passers-by, daring them to pop in just for one. This is a sister establishment to The Jolly Butchers in Stoke Newington and it shares many of the same virtues but being south of the river, it's just that touch more stylish, a little cooler.

The Crown and Anchor has recently been joined in Brixton by a new Craft Beer Co., but it has more than enough swagger to hold its own. Brixton's first beer venue is well-placed to remain Brixton's best beer venue.

THE UNION TAVERN

45 Woodfield Road W9 2BA
Tel: 020 7286 1886
Online: union-tavern.co.uk
@union_tavern
Mon-Thurs: 12pm - 11pm
Fri & Sat: 12pm - 12am
Sun: 12pm - 10.30pm

MONCADA BREWERY

Unit 5, Grand Union Centre, West Row W10 5AS
Tel: 07795 511 505
Online: moncadabrewery.co.uk
@MoncadaBrewery
What to try: Notting Hill Amber

THE DEFECTOR'S WELD

170 Uxbridge Road W12 8AA
Tel: 020 8749 0008
Online: defectors-weld.com
@defectorsweld
Mon-Thurs: 11am - 12am
Fri: 12pm - 2am
Sun: 12pm - 11pm

THE DUCHESS OF CAMBRIDGE

320 Goldhawk Road, Ravenscourt Park W6 0XF
Tel: 020 8834 7336
Online: theduchessofcambridgepub.com
@duchesspubw6
Mon-Thurs: 12pm - 11.30pm
Fri & Sat: 12pm -12am
Sun: 12pm - 10.30pm

FULLER'S

The Griffin Brewery, Chiswick Lane South W4 2QB
Tel: 020 8996 2000
Online: fullers.co.uk
@London_Pride
What to try: Fuller's ESB

THE BOTANIST

3-5 Kew Green, Richmond TW9 3AA
Tel: 020 8948 4838
Online: thebotanistkew.com
@_TheBotanistkew
Mon-Thurs: 12pm - 11pm
Fri & Sat: 12pm -12am
Sun: 12pm - 10.30pm

THE SUSSEX ARMS

15 Staines Road, Twickenham TW2 5BG
Tel: 020 8947 468
Online: thesussexarmstwickenham.co.uk
@thesussexarms
Mon-Sat: 12pm - 11pm
Sun: 12pm - 10.30pm

THE TRAFALGAR

200 Kings Road SW3 5XP
Tel: 020 7349 1831
Online: thetrafalgarchelsea.co.uk
Mon & Tues: 12pm - 11pm
Weds-Fri: 12pm - 12am
Sat: 11am - 12am
Sun: 12pm - 10.30pm

SAMBROOK'S BREWERY

Unit 1 & 2 Yelverton Road, Battersea SW11 3QG
Tel: 020 7228 0598
Online: sambrooksbrewery.co.uk
@sambrookale
What to drink: Wandle

BATTERSEA MESS & MUSIC HALL

49 Lavender Gardens, Clapham SW11 1DJ
Tel: 020 7223 6927
Online: batterseamessandmusichall.com
@MessandMusic
Mon-Weds: 4pm - 11pm
Thurs & Fri: 4pm - 12am
Sat: 12pm - 12am
Sun: 12pm - 10.30pm

DRAFT HOUSE - NORTHCOTE

94 Northcote Road SW11 6QW
Tel: 020 79241814
Online: drafthouse.co.uk
@drafthouseuk
Mon-Fri: 12pm - 11pm
Sat: 10am - 11pm
Sun: 10am - 10.30pm

CITIZEN SMITH

160 Putney High Street SW15 1RS
Tel: 020 8780 2235
Online: citizensmithbar.co.uk
@citizensmithsw
Mon: 4pm - 11pm
Tue & Weds: 12pm - 11pm
Thurs: 12pm -12am
Fri & Sat: 12pm - 2am   **Sun:** 12pm -11pm

BY THE HORNS

25 Summerstown, Wandsworth SW17 0BQ
Tel: 020 3417 7338
Online: bythehorns.co.uk
@bythehornsbrew
What to drink: Lambeth Walk porter

CRAFT BEER CO.

11-13 Brixton Station Road SW9 8PD
Online: thecraftbeerco.com
@CraftBeerCoSW9
Mon-Weds: 4pm - 11pm
Thurs: 4pm - 12am
Fri & Sat: 12pm - 3am
Sun: 12pm - 10.30pm

THE HOPE

48 West Street, Carshalton SM5 2PR
Tel: 020 8240 1255
Online: hopecarshalton.co.uk
@RowanTheHope
Mon-Sat: 12pm - 11pm
Sun: 12pm - 10.30pm

THE HISTORY OF
LONDON BREWING

by
Will Hawkes

When Young's departed London in 2006, it seemed like another sad milestone in the story of London's decline as a brewing powerhouse. It left the capital – a city where so many of the world's great beer styles were created – with two medium-sized breweries (Fuller's and Meantime) and a handful of pubs which made their own beer. While much of the rest of Britain enjoyed a microbrewery boom, London seemed oddly content to trade in its enviable heritage for a glass of nondescript Pinot Grigio or a fruit-based cocktail.

This was particularly sad because in the 18th and early 19th centuries there was no city on earth that could match London for beer. It was here that beer styles like porter, stout and India Pale Ale – perhaps *the* key craft-beer style – were born, and breweries like Whitbread, Barclay Perkins, Truman's and Courage were well known around the world. Beer was the drink that fuelled the greatest city on earth, the liquid that oiled the wheels of the largest empire the world has ever seen.

Indeed, London beer's greatest era dawned as Britain's empire-building days began in earnest. London's brewing history goes back many centuries (the City of London's Brewer's Guild was founded in 1342) but it was in the 18th century that its golden age began. By the middle of that century many of London's numerous breweries (there were 190 in 1700) were brewing a new beer that was to become synonymous with the city:

TRUMAN'S DRAY MEN

porter. This dark, moreishly bitter beer (a beer, not an ale: at that time the former included hops, unlike the latter) developed out of the brown beer most brewers of that era made: they added more hops in order to compete with the bitter, paler beers that were coming into fashion during the early years of the 18th century.

But porter - so named due to its popularity with those men who worked to unload ships on the river and carry goods around the city - would not have been such a smash hit had it not been for one key factor: it was easier and cheaper to make than other beers and ales. It could be fermented at a higher temperature, meaning it could be made when it was too hot to make other beers, and in larger vessels (which generated higher temperatures) too.

It was matured in giant vats, which led to tragedy in 1814 at Henry Meux's brewery in St Giles (close to where Tottenham Court Road meets Oxford Street today). Thirty-two tonnes of porter were sent spilling through the east wall of the brewery when a twenty-foot-high vat burst; the beer flooded out into the tightly-packed working-class homes around the brewery and eight people (all women and children; it was early evening and the men were still at work) were killed.

By then, porter had become famous around the world - and it was brewed around the world, too. George Washington got his porter from a brewer called Robert Hare in Philadelphia, for example. It's biggest contribution to today's beer drinkers, though, might have been its popularity in Dublin, where it made the fortune of Guinness, originally an ale brewer. It begat stout, which under Guinness's banner is still much-loved around the world.

Stout as we know it today, though, is a different beast to that made in 18th-century London. Back then, stout just meant *strong*. It was only by the early years of Queen Victoria's reign that it was popularly understood to mean *strong porter*. Perhaps the most interesting (and strongest) form of the beer was Imperial Russian Stout, initially brewed by Thrale's at the Anchor Brewery on the South side of the Thames and exported to the Baltic states and Russia from the late 18th century onwards. It was called imperial because it was intended for the court of Catherine II and it was (and still is) strong: typically 9 per cent and upwards.

Imperial Russian Stout is a beer style that, given its powerful, complex flavour, has inevitably become popular with American and British craft brewers, but the original – Thrale's – exists to this day (sort of). Thrale's Brewery became Barclay Perkins which, in turn, became Courage in 1955. The beer was produced until 1994, when Courage – who had looked increasingly disinterested – decided enough was enough. A sad end to a great story? Not quite. Wells and Young's now own the rights to Courage Imperial Russian Stout and they brought out a new version last year. That all

FULLER'S BREWING TEAM c.1908

of the first batch went to the US demonstrates that this famous London beer is now, sadly, more welcome across the pond.

Another beer much-loved in the US is India Pale Ale, so named because it was originally brewed for export to India. London's third great beer style, it emerged during the 19th century. The first use of the expression came in 1835, when the Bow brewer Hodgson's used it in an advert, but it was certainly popular before then – by 1844, Hodgson's was able to claim that it's beer had been 'held in high repute in India for nearly a century'.

It was not an entirely new beer: it was a version of a special October brew that was pale and more heavily-hopped than most beers. It was the lengthy journey to the subcontinent that transformed it into something special: when it arrived in India it had a remarkable depth and sophistication that delighted those Britons living in the Empire's most significant colony.

Between 1700 and 1850, London's brewers transformed the way Britons - and much of the world - consumed beer, but by the end of that era the first signs of its decline were evident. The rise of the railways had put London within the orbit of big regional brewers, in particular those of Burton. This Midlands town enjoyed a crucial advantage: its water. Being rich in calcium sulphate (a flavour enhancer), it is perfect for brewing highly-hopped pale ales. As a result, Burton brewers like Bass and Allsopp's became Britain's biggest names. Indeed, many brewers – wherever they are – now 'Burtonise' their water in order to replicate that effect.

But while the age of innovation was over, London still had many large breweries and there were still significant changes to come. Take the way the rise of mild ale (which, in those days, just meant a young or fresh beer rather than a weak, mildly-flavoured one) in the early years of the 19th century changed the London scene. Many brewers that had previously only brewed porter turned to mild, and new brewers emerged (like Courage) that focused on mild ale.

By the end of the 19th century, porter had lost much of its previous significance and an era of contraction and consolidation was well underway. In 1941 Whitbread brewed porter for the final time, and by 1952 there were just twenty-five breweries left in the capital. By 1976 that was down to nine; Courage's brewery by Tower Bridge closed in 1981 and Truman's huge plant by Brick Lane followed in 1989. Then, in 2006, Young's Brewery closed.

That looked to be almost that, notwithstanding the emergence in the late 1970s of the Firkin brewpub chain. The Firkins themselves are gone now but in the last few years, a new breed of brewer has helped to reignite the dying embers of a great brewing tradition. There are now more than two dozen breweries in the Old Smoke and counting. There are also perhaps a dozen planned breweries that should be making beer by the start of next year, including the new Truman Brewery that has been re-established in Hackney Wick.

Inspired by tradition but also, crucially, the American craft beer revolution, brewers have once again captured the imagination of Londoners. London may have created IPA, but it's the American version – brewed with New World hops – that is most common in the city's craft beer focused pubs. Most of the best new brewers follow the American model, in the process aping their forebears: after many years when beer in England became weaker and blander, it is being brewed to pack a punch again. Those legendary 18th-century porter brewers would recognise a few kindred spirits among London's current beer scene.

That's because some of London's breweries are truly world-class: Fuller's may well be the most well-respected traditional cask ale producer around, while The Kernel has earned a cast-iron reputation for high-quality pale ales and dark beers that magnificently evoke London's brewing past. Each new brewery that opens adds to the richness of a vibrant scene: pubs are opening almost every week – particularly in Hackney, which surely deserves the moniker 'craft beer borough' – that offer their customers a truly world-class selection. Beer in London is back, and the future looks good. It should taste pretty good, too.

FURTHER READING:

'Amber, Gold and Black: The History of Britain's Great Beers', by Martyn Cornell. Published by The History Press.

'Hops and Glory: One Man's Search for the beer that built the British Empire' by Pete Brown. Published by Pan.

LONDON BREWERS' ALLIANCE

by

Phil Lowry

The London Brewers' Alliance came about as a result of a small group of brewers coming together to share and collaborate. There are few things that are more fun for a brewer than hanging out with your fellow brewers. Bringing together all of London's brewers was just an extension of that - it seemed like it would be enjoyable, so we did it.

It started in April 2010, soon after Steve Skinner and I had begun brewing at Brew Wharf in Borough. I had recently met Evin O'Riordain, who was in the process of setting up The Kernel nearby, close to Tower Bridge. All three of us came from the same homebrewing background and we had the same attitude: let's enjoy ourselves and make some good beer. If you're going to be sweating your arse off in a brewery, I figured, you might as well have fun doing it.

The initial impetus to extend that and get in touch with London's other breweries (there were nine at this stage) was equally simple: to have fun, sure, but also to learn. If you want to be a better brewer, it makes sense to learn from those who have been there and done it. I was also influenced by my experiences in San Francisco, a place that I had visited many times. There I had seen the camaraderie that exists amongst the Bay Area brewers and how the San Francisco Brewer's Guild had helped to raise the profile of beer in the region. It seemed to be a good model to follow and, having met most of my fellow London brewers, I knew they

were a decent bunch and would be amenable. Even so, the first time we got all the brewers round a table at the Brew Wharf, it was a real 'wow' moment. There were guys like John Keeling and Paddy Johnson from Fuller's in attendance and although it was just a get-together, having people like them there made it seem significant.

It was John, actually, who leant over towards me during the meal and said, "We should do this again." I suggested to him that we could get a more formal (but not too formal) organisation going, and he agreed. The idea was popular: it was a hugely positive evening and the energy in the room was amazing. The passion for beer in that room was so evident; I repeat, just amazing.

You need to be passionate to brew in London, though. It's a difficult place: land cost and rents are way above the norm and over recent years more breweries have closed than have opened. We could see, though, that the first shoots of a growing scene were starting to emerge. The likes of Meantime and Sambrook's had established a real toehold - you could sense a change of mood. It was essential that we let Londoners know what was going on. There were three ways we decided to do that - with a showcase event, with a cooperatively brewed beer and with a film.

The latter was in some ways the hardest part: brewers aren't naturally the happiest in front of the camera and plenty of lines were forgotten along the way but it worked in the end and let people know what was happening, since it was tweeted and blogged about across the world.

The showcase was an inevitable extension of that. We wanted to show Londoners that there was great beer being made in their city and, furthermore, we wanted them to taste it. For me, working in a brewpub, it was easy to get close to the public but for Fuller's, or then new-boys Camden Town, it was great to see how much people appreciated their efforts. I think five kegs of Camden's beer were sold at that first showcase event in September 2010 - it was quite a hit!

Then there was the collaborative beer. We wanted to get something that was uniquely London into the hands of our customers so it was only right that we produced a porter. We took an old porter recipe, added a dash of Munich malt and dry-hopped it with American Liberty hops. I believe it was the first citywide collaborative brew in the UK. It was very London, but with a twist.

It was a great experience. We did all the brewing up at Redemption in Tottenham, which is run by Andy Moffat. He's one of the most hospitable, charitable and hard-working men you'll ever meet. The opportunity to work with other brewers and find out how they did things was not to be missed: I remember Tom Madeiros from Twickenham Ales, a well-travelled brewer, saying that he hadn't learnt so much in years.

This sort of collaborative effort, I believe, helps set new standards. If you're brewing in London, then you have to aim to be as good as Fuller's, so to spend a day brewing with John or Derek is priceless. After all, they've both been in charge of a brew house longer than I've been alive.

Following on from the success of our first attempts, we decided to make another collaborative brew the next year: an IPA brewed at Windsor & Eton. This was something of a hybrid between an old English IPA and a contemporary American-leaning type, and it too proved a success. In 2012 we've made an old-school stout - an 1800's recipe from beer historian Ron Pattinson's archives - at The Kernel's new larger space in Bermondsey. There were a crazy number of brewers all queuing up to help stir the mash in. Oddly, there were just two of us there to do the hard work of emptying the mash – perhaps the most laborious part of the process - under the sure hand of Derek from Fuller's.

The spirit of collaboration has extended beyond those London Brewers' Alliance beers, though. Take London Brick, a beer we first made up at Redemption with brewers from The Kernel, Zerodegrees, Brew Wharf and, from down in deepest Sussex, Dark Star's uber-cool head brewer Mark Tranter. It was a contemporary, hoppy, red-rye ale, and it has developed a bit of a cult following. Since then it has been brewed at The Kernel as Big Brick, at Brodie's as Brick and at Brew Wharf as Yellow Brick - all different versions of the original brew. Just recently, we have re-brewed it at The Kernel.

I think all of this gives an idea of what a co-operative, collegiate world brewing is. I am a firm believer in the idea of a "brewer's code": I love sharing knowledge, ideas, research and much besides over a glass of great beer. And, ultimately, animosity between brewers doesn't help anyone. I have never been to brewing school but brewers near and far have helped me get where I am and I hope I have helped wherever possible, too.

This is the key to craft beer: it's a philosophy more than anything else. It's about openness - to new ideas, to new friends, travel, sharing, creativity and respect. I am proud to be part of such a great movement. Long live London brewing.

WHERE TO BUY CRAFT BEER?

While craft beer pubs have proliferated over the past few months, it remains frustratingly difficult to find off-licenses with a decent selection of beer. Too many places still regard beer as something to swill rather than a drink that can more than compete with wine when it comes to complexity and variety of flavour.

Thankfully, things are changing. Whilst it would be an exaggeration to say that most Londoners are within walking distance of a good off-license, there are more and more bottle shops that have cottoned on to what's happening in the world of beer. Chief among them – and perhaps the most central-ish of all – is **Utobeer** (open Wed-Sat; Unit 24, Middle Row, Borough Market SE1 1TL; utobeer.co.uk) at Borough Market. Utobeer has a superb range of British, American, Belgian and German beers, plus plenty more besides. Prices reflect its location and the scarcity of some of these beers.

Somewhere to the South of Utobeer is **Mr Lawrence** (Tues-Sun; 391, Brockley Road SE4 2PH; mrlawrencewinemerchant.co.uk), which has become a bit of a mecca for South East London's growing band of craft beer lovers. The fact that The Kernel brewed a special beer to celebrate Mr Lawrence's 20th year in business in July 2012 tells you all you need to know about the respect in which this place is held. Indeed, if you're looking for The Kernel's beers, and you can't make it to the brewery on Saturday mornings, this should be your first port of call.

Also in South East London is **Theatre of Wine** (Sun-Sat; 75 Trafalgar Road, Greenwich, SE10 9TS; theatreofwine.com), which has a decent selection including some fairly rare beers from Britain and further afield. There's another, similarly good branch in Tufnell Park.

It's a surprise given the number of craft beer pubs in the area that East London doesn't have more decent off-licenses. Perhaps the pick of the bunch is **City Beverage Company** (Sun-Sat; 303 Old Street, Hoxton EC1V 9IA; citybeverage.co.uk) where, tucked away amidst an impressive array of wines, spirits and cigars, you'll find a tidy little selection of beer.

North London is somewhat better served. There's **Highbury Vintners** (Sun-Sat; 71 Highbury Park N5 1UA; highburyvintners.co.uk), another wine shop which also appreciates beer's charms, **Drinker's Paradise** (Sun-Sat; 129 Castlehaven Road, Kentish Town NW1 8SJ; drinkersparadise.co.uk), which seems to be particularly good on German beers, and **Kris Wines** (Sun-Sat; 394 York Way N7 9LW; kriswines.com). The latter is the pick: it's a veritable Aladdin's Cave of beer. You'll find stuff in here you didn't know was available in the UK.

South West London is the opposite of East London: some lacklustre pubs, three excellent beer shops. The first, **Drink of Fulham** (Tues-Sun; 349 Fulham Palace Road SW6 6TB; drinkoffulham.com), stocks beers you'll struggle to find elsewhere – a recent visit turned up Kentish brewer Old Dairy's Hop Top, a powerful imperial IPA, and Cantillon Iris, a Lambic beer that is hopped just before bottling to create a unique bitterness. Then there's the superb **Beer Boutique** (Sun-Sat; 134 Upper Richmond Road SW15 2SP; thebeerboutique.co.uk) in Putney, which has an airy elegance that might put you in mind of a high-end wine shop.

Finally, there's **Nelson Wines** down in Merton (Sun-Sat, only opens at 6pm in the week; 168 Merton High Street, Wimbledon SW19 1AZ; nelsonwines.com). The range is very decent and it's hard to miss, what with it being painted bright red.

BEER DICTIONARY

This list is, of course, far from comprehensive: it is intended to help newcomers to beer understand these terms more thoroughly. To find out more, we suggest seeking out The Oxford Companion to Beer.

GOLDEN ALE is exactly what it says: a beer that is golden in colour. Such beers have become increasingly popular over the past 20 years and tend to be well-hopped.

HAND PUMP is a device commonly used to serve real ale.

HELLS is a type of lager native to Bavaria. Like Pilsner in colour but less bitter.

HOPS are a plant commonly used to make beer bitter. They are grown around the world: like grapes, the same hop grown in a different part of the world can have very different flavours. In general, new world hops (like Citra from the US or Nelson Sauvin from New Zealand) tend to have bolder flavours than traditional British hops.

IPA is a strong, sometimes bracingly bitter version of pale ale. Most craft IPAs are American-style: very hoppy, bitter/sweetish, often with a citric, grapefruit character.

KEG BEERS are served by gas pressure. Despite what CAMRA might tell you, they don't have to be pasteurised: indeed, real craft examples aren't.

LAGER is a beer type that, at its best, should be clean and crisp but flavoursome, too. It is distinguished from ale by the fact that it is fermented and conditioned at low temperatures.

MALT is the main ingredient in beer. It is grain seeds – generally barley, but often wheat and other grains too – that have been partially germinated and then dried.

PALE ALE covers any number of different beers, from fairly sweetish cask bitters to extremely hop-forward West Coast style ales. In terms of colour, it could be anything from copper to golden. Generally, the modern craft pale ales are hoppy and light in colour.

PILSNER is the most famous type of lager. It is golden and was first brewed in Pilsen in the Czech Republic, hence the name. Some versions can be noticeably bitter.

PORTER/STOUT is the traditional beer style of London. Nowadays there is little difference between porter and stout (and perhaps there never was): both beers are dark and often have a bitter, roasted character. American versions tend to have a stronger hop character than British porters and stouts.

REAL ALE is a type of unpasteurised beer which is served from a cask by hand pump, hopefully (but all too rarely) at cellar temperature. The term was coined by CAMRA in the 1970s during their battle against the blandification of British beer.

SPARKLING is a method whereby an attachment on the nozzle of a beer engine fires air into the pint, creating a thick head and smoother mouthfeel.

SPONTANEOUS FERMENTATION

is a process whereby a beer is exposed to (and fermented by) the wild yeast in the environment. Most beers, by contrast, are fermented with cultivated yeast. The Lambics of Belgium are produced by spontaneous fermentation: a classic like Cantillon Gueuze should be lemon-dry, sour and extremely moreish.

YEAST is the unsung hero of brewing. It transforms hopped wort (the mixture of malt, hops and water) into beer. It often plays a key role in the flavour of the beer, too.

ACKNOWLEDGEMENTS

Will Hawkes would like to thank Claudine, Evin O'Riordain, Phil Lowry, Jasper Cuppaidge, Peter Holt, Andy Moffat, Camilla Brown, James Gordon-MacIntosh, Alastair Hook, James Brodie, Glyn Roberts, Logan Plant, Joseph Ryan and Fi Collett.

In addition, the publisher would also like to thank Derek Lamberton, James Lambie, Robin Sykes, Luca Sage, Adam Driver, James Morgan and all of those that made the publication of this book possible.

www.bluecrowmedia.com

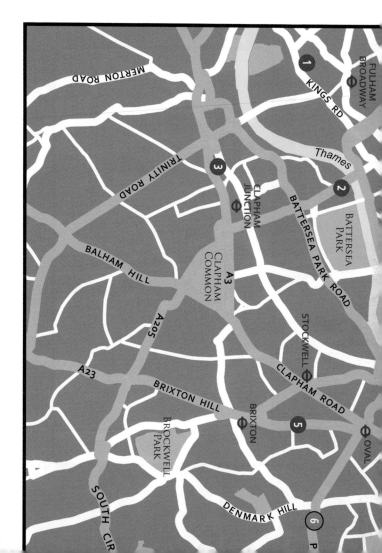

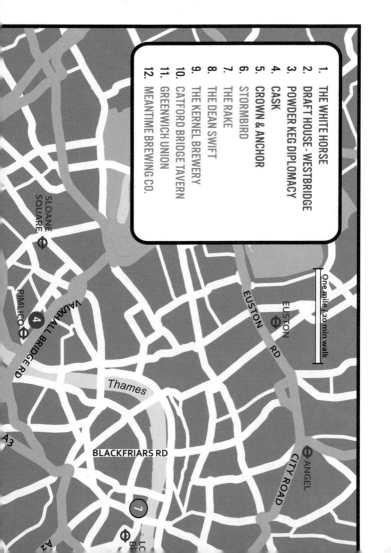

1. THE WHITE HORSE
2. DRAFT HOUSE - WESTBRIDGE
3. POWDER KEG DIPLOMACY
4. CASK
5. CROWN & ANCHOR
6. STORMBIRD
7. THE RAKE
8. THE DEAN SWIFT
9. THE KERNEL BREWERY
10. CATFORD BRIDGE TAVERN
11. GREENWICH UNION
12. MEANTIME BREWING CO.

One mile / 20 min walk

SLOANE
SQUARE

PIMLICO

VAUXHALL BRIDGE RD

EUSTON

EUSTON
RD

Thames

BLACKFRIARS RD

CITY ROAD

ANGEL

A3

A2

LO
BR

Craft Beer London is your indispensible guide to the finest craft beer pubs, bars and breweries in the capital. Featuring expert reviews, detailed maps, listings and articles by some of craft beer's foremost exponents, this book will guide you on your search for the best beer in London and serve as a faithful drinking companion on your travels.

Vespertine PRESS

ISBN: 978-0-9566582-3-4

RRP £10